Learning without School

Learning without School
Home Education

Ross Mountney

Jessica Kingsley Publishers
London and Philadelphia

First published in 2009
by Jessica Kingsley Publishers
116 Pentonville Road
London N1 9JB, UK
and
400 Market Street, Suite 400
Philadelphia, PA 19106, USA

www.jkp.com

Library of Congress Cataloging in Publication Data
Mountney, Ross.
    Learning without school : home education / Ross Mountney.
        p. cm.
    Includes bibliographical references and index.
    ISBN 978-1-84310-685-2 (pb : alk. paper) 1. Home schooling. 2. Education--Parent participa-
tion. I. Title.
    LC40.M68 2009
    371.04'2--dc22
                                                                2008024512

British Library Cataloguing in Publication Data
A CIP catalogue record for this book is available from the British Library

ISBN 978 1 84310 685 2

Contents

Introduction

There is a secret many parents are unaware of: children can be educated without going to school. In fact, it's not really a secret, just a little known fact that going to school is not compulsory. It is *education* that is compulsory.

This book is all about a non-school approach to education and to children enjoying their learning. So although it may be about education, it is not about schools or teaching or how to make geniuses of your children, even if with home educating this is sometimes the result!

This book is simply here to help you help your children learn. To help you show them what a wonderful experience education is and how it enables them to become the people they need and want to be. And it includes important truths about all children's learning, whether they are in school or not.

Many, many parents are dissatisfied with schools, not only with the education they provide but the environment children have to endure in order to be educated. And many are also dissatisfied with the narrow focus of schools towards mass qualification rather than the personal development of the individual.

Home educators are the parents who do something about it. They remove their children from school and create a tailor-made education; one better suited to their children's needs; one that offers a comfortable climate in which to learn. In doing so their children develop not only their academic standard but also their personal, social and life skills, and a fundamental life-purpose for education.

This book describes what home education is and how to make this happen. It shows why it happens and has stories from parents already home educating. It is full of ideas and tips if you want to give it a go, offers encouragement and support if you're already doing so, and contains an inspirational philosophy of education for everyone else.

This book is dedicated to all those people who made it possible; to those families who have shared their children's education with me and made such a great contribution, to the pioneering families who have gone before and showed us the home education route, and those special few closest to me who have given so much support. Thank you.

Chapter 1

What Is Home Education and Why Do People Do It?

This chapter is a complete introduction to home education for those who are not already familiar with it. In it we will look at the following issues:

What is home education?

Is it legal?

Frequently asked questions and a few quick answers

Why do people home educate?

Why did we home educate? – A personal story

The advantages of home education

A brief word about friends

The disadvantages

What you need to home educate

What is home education?

Home education is a very different, workable and successful approach to learning that some parents are choosing for their children instead of school. Simply defined, home education is when parents take the opportunity of full responsibility for their children's education without sending them to school.

Parents do this in a variety of ways, mostly using the home as a base, but also by taking advantage of the resources within their community, resources like museums, libraries, galleries, sports centres, and by interacting with other families and groups of home educators, going on field trips and visiting places of interest. They use a readily available supply of books to help them, plus the Internet. Some parents use tutors and other professionals and there are always other parents with specialist skills, groups, clubs and classes available. A few schools are flexible and allow home educators to use their resources.

It is an open-ended and variable approach to learning that is proving to give children a broad and deep education, often quite different from that which many of them would receive in school. It generally develops children who are extremely motivated, self-confident, sociable and intelligent, who have a wide variety of life skills and who successfully go on to higher education or into work.

✳

There are already thousands of families educating their children out of school.

✳

I have two children who are now 14 and 16 and have been mainly home educated. We first began after my eldest had been in school for a term and became really unhappy. Neither the school environment, nor the social environment within it suited him at all – he wanted to explore, play and enjoy and was expected to sit an awful lot. In the playground he was being badly bullied, which the school tried to keep from me and refused to discuss. One morning, whilst preparing to pull my once-happy child down the street bawling, I just stopped, turned around and went home. I could not believe I had never done so before. It was like a huge weight was simply removed and we begun our new life, really just a continuation of the life we had before it was interrupted.

Parent of two children, home educating for ten years

Is it legal?

This is the first question people always ask and the answer is *yes*.

The best way to explain how it's legal is to start with an important fact that most parents are not aware of. Most parents think that schools are responsible for the education of their children and they are bound by law to send them there. Most parents think that school is compulsory. But this is not the case.

*

Education is compulsory.

School is not.

*

School is *not* compulsory and parents are not bound by law to send their children there. Parents are bound by law to *educate* their children but that doesn't necessarily have to be in school.

Parents have always been the ones responsible for their children's education, by law. It's just that most parents hand their children over to schools for that to happen, as they are expected to do. But the overall responsibility still remains with the parents, even when the children are in school. Parents have always had the option of *not* sending their children to school, although most people are unaware of that fact as it is not something that is widely known.

It is just the same as parents always having had the option to send their children to schools other than state schools and educate them privately. That option has always been there and some parents use it. Home education could just be seen as another way of educating a child privately, except that parents choose not to use a school to do so.

In England and Wales it is the Education Act of 1996, within section 7, that refers to parents' right to educate their children out of schools if they so wish. (In Scotland the law is worded rather differently but it still allows the option of home educating.) This has developed from the Education Act of 1944 onwards. It states that

> the parent of every child of compulsory school age shall cause him to receive efficient full-time education suitable to
>
> a) his age, ability and aptitude and
>
> b) any special educational needs he may have,
>
> either by regular attendance at school or otherwise.

It is the 'otherwise' bit that gives parents the option and the right to home educate. It is also where Education Otherwise, the largest organisation to support home educators, takes their name from. Educating otherwise than at school could mean privately educating through private tutors, home educating, or any other form of education that is suitable.

The interpretation of the words of the law, for example: 'efficient full-time education suitable to his age, ability and aptitude', is very flexible. It allows home educators room to give their children an education that suits their individuality, their personality and their special gifts and needs. Parents already home educating find that they can easily incorporate these legal requirements within quite a wide range of educational approaches, styles and practices.

If you want to find out more about the legalities they are all explained on the website of Education Otherwise (EO): www.education-otherwise.org.

Next we'll look at other pressing questions that parents always ask about home education.

Frequently asked questions and a few quick answers

- Do you need to be a teacher?
- Do you need to follow the National Curriculum?
- Do you need to do tests?
- Do you need to have a timetable?
- Do you need to have a 'schoolroom'?
- Do you need to do 'school' at home?
- Do you have to have a degree, A levels, or GCSEs in order to home educate?
- Do children end up with no friends?
- Do children turn out to be thick and stupid?
- Does it cost lots of money?
- Do you have to be rich?

The quick, simple and honest answer to all of these is *no*! But we will look at them all in depth throughout the rest of the book along with many of the other questions that parents always ask. Questions such as:

- How do parents start home educating?
- How do home educated children learn?
- How do home educated children find friends and become sociable?
- What about curriculum, subjects and timetables?
- What about tests, exams and qualifications?
- What is life like for a home educating family?

- What about children with 'learning difficulties' and 'special needs'?
- Where do children who have been home educated end up?

These are the questions we will discuss throughout the rest of the book, chapter by chapter. What many parents ask is why families home educate in the first place. This is what is discussed in the next section.

Why do people home educate?

> My decision to home educate came about mainly as our child was so lively and inquisitive. I could not imagine him sitting quietly in a class doing things by the clock and did not want his natural thirst for knowledge dampened down by having to follow the National Curriculum. I feel one mistake I made at this point was to draw my son's attention to the fact he was now school age and we had to start 'learning' as that was what was expected of us. This was of course what we had been doing all along with no pressure and I regret 'formalising' that learning as it spoilt the natural flow. With my two subsequent children I haven't felt the same pressure to produce results and consequently the path has been much smoother for them.
>
> Parent of three children, home educating for seven years

There are as many different reasons why families choose not to send their children to school as there are different families and lifestyles. And many, many very ordinary families home educate. It is not just people who are rich, elitist or very 'alternative', as some people suppose.

These ordinary families want the same simple things for their children as any family, as you or I do. They want their children to thrive and be happy and healthy. They want their children to develop personal and academic skills that will be of value throughout their life. They want their children to gain the qualifications they need to do that. They want their children to become well equipped with the skills and knowledge needed to go forward into work. But not all families feel that schools fulfil those criteria for each of their children. And it's those families who are choosing to home educate.

Some families intend to home educate from the outset, making that decision before they even send their children to school. Some families encounter problems with their children being in school and remove them to

We started home educating because school clearly did not suit our eldest son. After two years he had changed from a bright, happy, inquisitive pre-schooler into a child who seemed constantly worried, was switched off from learning, and who scarcely ever completed a week of school because of a succession of head-aches, sore throats and stomach upsets. Within a fortnight of removing him from school he was back to his 'normal' self, and our whole family was much happier. We had originally decided to try home education for a year, but it soon became clear that the relaxed style of learning we were able to provide was much more suitable for him and his brothers, who have never attended school.

Parent of three children, home educating for ten years

continue their education at home. Some families have both children in school and children they are educating at home. It varies from family to family, just as the school experience varies from family to family.

The idea of school is brilliant. The idea that children have the opportunity to learn alongside others, with adults who have greater knowledge and experience than they have, in a safe and stimulating environment, is brilliant. Many schools and many teachers are brilliant.

Trouble is, not *all* schools are like that, whatever the ideal might be. And, anyway, not all children fit that approach. Not all children learn in an ideal way. Not all children are able to learn effectively in that environment. And not all adults in schools treat children in the way we might wish them to be treated.

Schools, teachers and all school-like institutions have enormous amounts of pressure put upon them in today's educational climate. Pressure to get the children to achieve. Pressure to please parents. Pressure to please government officials. Pressure to cope with children who perhaps have not been parented in a way that makes them particularly nice people to be with! Pressure to fulfil the demands of a National Curriculum. And all this pressure has created a climate within schools that some parents find is not what they want for their children. Not educationally. Not personally, either.

When you think about it, the likelihood of one educational system suiting every individual child is pretty small. When you think about children, when you think about their diverse and wonderful characteristics and personalities, their varied and individual learning needs, how different they all are, you can perhaps begin to understand how there might be a need for variable educational approaches.

Because going to a school is just one approach to an education, although we tend not to realise that. And the large numbers of children being taught in schools govern both the education on offer and the way in which that education is implemented. Look outside of that, as parents who home educate begin to do, and it becomes apparent that there are actually all sorts of other different and workable approaches to an education.

Basically, most parents home educate because they want a different approach, because schools, and the education provided there, are not what the parents want for their children, or just did not suit their children and they did not thrive there. As awareness of home education as an option grows more families are deciding upon home education from the outset.

Here are some of the reasons why parents opt not to send their children to school in the first place.

- They do not want their very young children to start formalised learning too early.
- They do not like the idea of large groups of children with only small numbers of adults.
- They are unhappy with a set curriculum and want the opportunity for a child to develop their particular interests or gifts.
- They do not feel that the educational system suits their child's learning needs.
- They are unhappy with the kind of relationships they see within some schools, e.g. bullying.
- They are unhappy about the behaviour in some schools.
- Their child is unhappy with larger groups of children.
- There's not enough opportunity for individual attention.
- They want a different education for their children.
- They want a different kind of lifestyle from that promoted by school.

Here are some of the reasons why parents remove their children from school after they have started there.

- Their children are failing to achieve.
- Their children are unwell or unhappy.

- The children become withdrawn or there are adverse effects in their behaviour and personality after starting school.

- They are unhappy with the staff.

- They are unhappy with the way children are treated in school.

- The children are being bullied and nothing has been done about it.

- They don't like the behaviour in school.

- They find the set curriculum restrictive.

- Not enough attention is paid to creative skills.

- Not enough attention is paid to basic skills.

- There is not enough opportunity for the child to develop his personal strengths.

- Dissatisfaction with the atmosphere in schools.

- Failure to address particular educational needs.

The list varies and grows from family to family.

You only have to bring up the subject of education within any group of parents to know it is a minefield of worry for all of us. Most parents at some time have to deal with heart-wrenching anxieties or problems their children are facing. These problems seem to fall into several main categories:

- Educational achievement or failure to achieve as expected.

- Failure to thrive and diminished happiness, health and well-being within the child.

- Unsatisfactory relationships within the school environment.

- Dissatisfaction with the climate within schools.

- Sometimes, of course, there's no problem at all – it's a lifestyle choice.

Most of the reasons why parents home educate fall within these groups or a collection of them. It all boils down to either the parents or the children being unhappy about what's going on in schools.

Now, you may think: what's happiness got to do with it? But

✳

Happiness is essential for education.

And they *can* work together.

✳

It is important because basically *unhappy children don't learn well*. They don't thrive and they don't reach their potential.

Some children are very happy in school; they thrive, establish good relationships and learn well, achieve great things, get good grades. Some children are desperately unhappy in school; they don't thrive and they don't learn as well as they might. And there are many children in between.

My son had a good reception year at school, but the rest of primary school was mixed. On numerous occasions I considered pulling him out, but then he would have a year with a teacher whom he liked so we lurched through the system. I would say that the problems were the results of clashes of personality between him and some teachers and the lack of opportunity for him to have a 'voice'. He lives in a household where children have a voice.

Within six weeks of starting secondary school I was hauled in about his behaviour. Our local secondary school would be seen as 'excellent'. It is a high ranking state secondary school with fantastic academic results. Along with this is an institutional arrogance. I had a history with the school in that my eldest son had been chucked out at 16. Interestingly he is now one of the youngest 'rising stars' in his field – education! I battled on with the school as my son had great opportunities to play music – his gift is popular music, at school he was able to form and work with bands and there were numerous performing opportunities. This is what kept him there, but by year eight I was getting daily phone calls and he was forever on detention or being internally or externally excluded. I felt I was dealing with too much testosterone in the male teachers whose main aim was to 'crack' him and force him to comply. My son was never overtly rude to a teacher nor were there any complaints about his school work. It was his 'attitude' because he challenged teachers. Because of his music he tried to stick it out; this lasted about two weeks and I withdrew him from school.

I write this because the process that led to our eventual decision to 'go it alone' may be useful for other parents. I get the impression that a number of parents are less sure about continuing to home educate at secondary level. In the end I felt that school was ruining my son and fostering a sense of low self-esteem in him. He felt he was 'bad' and the school was 'normal society' and 'right'. And I feared he would play the role they had labelled him with.

Parent of one child, home educated for three years

Home educators find that children can achieve good grades and enjoy a happy learning life without suffering and without school if needs be, and they can still successfully go forward into work. That's why so many parents are choosing to do it.

And that's probably the main reason why we chose to do it too.

Why did we home educate? – A personal story

We didn't plan to home educate. After all, I'd been working in primary schools for ten years and was supposedly pro-school. Having said that, there were quite a few procedures that were beginning to make me feel uncomfortable.

When we became parents and saw what bright, inquisitive learning machines children are we couldn't believe it. No one who's ever brought up a toddler could dispute the fact that they want to learn. How do we know that? Well, they're pressing buttons, in every cupboard, opening every drawer, picking up, handling and chewing everything in attempts – no, not to annoy you even though it seems like that – but to find out about their world. They're desperate to know about everything. I expect you noticed that nearly every sentence starts with a 'why'!

So when mine were young I asked myself, if all children start off like this, like all the toddlers at the pre-school group seemed to be, where do those dis-enchanted teenagers come from, the ones who've lost all interest in learning who I see standing round the streets bunking off school?

When the time came we dutifully sent our bright little blooms off to school. Then, over the next few years we watched those bright little blooms fade. We saw the smile die off their faces. We watched them contract illness after illness. We saw the heavy weight of the National Curriculum bear them down when they were not old enough even to know what the National Curriculum was. And we tried very hard to keep a positive view of what seemed to be very negative relationships between the people in schools, both children and adults. Even worse, the children soon adopted a very negative attitude to learning. There were two catalysts that pushed us into removing the children from school.

Our eldest was the most giggly, happy infant anyone could be blessed to have. During her four years in school she eventually learned not to giggle any more. She only wore a heavy solemn little face, even at home. Had she grown out of giggling? Not only that, she was constantly ill with minor infections. I asked one teacher whether she thought she was happy in school. The teacher replied that she had noticed a change; my child never smiled any more. I was so sad when I heard that. Did all her school years have to be like this?

Our youngest was only in school one year before we felt we had to do something. She was already being 'kept in' for not finishing her writing, which we didn't feel was appropriate at four years of age. If ever there was a child who needed to be outdoors she was it. When she wasn't outdoors she used to tinkle on the piano and wanted piano lessons. After she'd been in school a while that all changed. She said that now she didn't want piano lessons because she 'hated learning'. I was so shocked.

We decided to do something. We looked around at other schools but our location did not offer a great deal of variety. So we gave the children the option to learn at home. Eight years later we're still at it, although the eldest has now gone on to further education at college. We did ask them several times if they wanted to return to school. We haven't had a 'yes' yet!

But what we have had is our happy, smiling children back. Giggling wasn't just something our daughter grew out of; she's a teenager now and she's still giggling. The stress of school just changed her personality. It took a year to get the giggle back. And she has had few infectious illnesses since. Our other daughter has got back her investigative spirit and interest in learning. She has plenty of time outside even as a teenager and has returned to her music. School killed her ambition to learn to do anything. I hate to think what would have happened to her if she had been continually 'kept in' as it looked like she might be destined to be.

My story is fairly typical of many home educating families. Many home educating families find that children's spirits don't need to be quashed or 'kept in' in order for children to learn things. Many home educating families believe that children's spirits can be used as an *asset* to their education, rather than considered disruptive as so many children are labelled, for there are all kinds of ways to learn.

We decided that what we wanted was a little less emphasis on the academic skills, although these are of course vitally important. But alongside them we wanted more emphasis on individual growth and development, the opportunity to make use of individual strengths and talents. We also wanted less time spent on test passing and more on proactive learning. We felt that home education could give our children a better opportunity to develop as individuals, and at the same time keep our children interested in learning.

The advantage of home educating is that it is all about the *individual* child and what suits them best. Let's look at some of the other advantages now.

The advantages of home education

At this point it might help to imagine something. Imagine going to buy a new outfit. A new outfit that's going to suit you, exactly you, whoever you are and whatever shape you are. So off you go to the shops to buy your outfit but all you can find is a size 16.5. Not an 8 or a 12, a 20 or a 24. Not a petite, or a tall, or a large or a long leg. Just *one* size; a size 16.5.

How restrictive that would be. There'd be no alternative if you couldn't find an outfit to fit – you'd have to have one tailor-made, just for you.

The best type of education anyone could have would be tailor-made to suit their needs and their personality. In schools, with the constraints they are under, it is difficult to achieve that. But home educating can give a child exactly what they individually need. And, unlike the tailored outfit, it doesn't cost the earth.

✳

Home education can be tailor-made to suit the individual child.

✳

Nearly all the other advantages with home educating fall under that same umbrella of giving the child an education that suits them and their needs. Here are some of them:

- *Learning speed.* There need be no age restrictions on when a child has to learn something. They can learn at their own pace in their own time.

- *Learning styles.* There need be no restrictions on the style of education a family might want to adopt like perhaps a more practical one, or one involving more discussion or investigation.

- *No bullying.* There is *never* any occasion when a child would have to endure being bullied.

- *Learning structure.* There need be no limits on the learning structure in terms of work schemes, days, timetables, etc.

- *Personal preferences.* Families can work in a way that suits their child best like using the computer more instead of books, working late afternoon instead of early morning.

- *Personal development.* Parents can tailor their child's education to suit their personal development rate, e.g. they can have time to spend longer on a subject or area if they need to, or can move onto another one quickly without having to wait for others to catch up.

- *Interaction.* Each child gets to choose who they want to learn, work and play with rather than being with a set group.

- *No teacher favouritism or worse!* The child does not have to put up with a teacher who favours others or who picks on them.

- *Attention to the child.* The child gets the opportunity for plenty of individual attention and learning support.

- *Encouraging relationships.* Learning can always be based on positive encouragement. Children can learn without sarcasm, ridicule, humiliation or a sense of failure which some may experience in some schools.

- *Comfortable learning environment.* The child can learn in an environment where they feel comfortable and confident, both of which have an impact on the child's achievement.

- *Self-motivation.* Children can learn to be in charge of their own education and this tends to develop self-motivation.

- *More options.* The family can choose what to study and when to study. So they can study the subjects that suit the child. They can also choose what tests or exams to do – or not to do if it's preferred.

- *Increased social development.* Children mix in groups where there are high proportions of adults to children, which increases the development of social skills and maturity.

- *Increased confidence and self-esteem.* Home educated children generally seem to have more self-confidence and higher self-esteem than some of their school peers.

- *Greater opportunity for learning in the wider environment.* Things like field trips, visits and workshops.

✳

Best of all: there is no need for a child to suffer.

✳

These are the main advantages. There are also many hidden advantages too that have an effect on family life. Things like: being able to take family holidays when it suits. Not to mention they're cheaper in term times and the beach is quiet.

Home educators find that the release from school can sometimes increase the togetherness within a family and relationships improve. Yes – even with the teenagers sometimes! There are of course no school runs, no packed lunches (only on field trips – there can be lots of those) and no uniform to buy. And the greatest benefit of all is that it is the *parents*, not the teacher, who get to see the child blossom.

A brief word about friends

There's a whole chapter (4) about children making friends and learning social skills but as it is such a big concern for parents, especially for anyone consider- ing home education, I thought it important to mention here that home educated children have friends just like all children do. I know quite a lot of home educators. I don't know *any* home educated child who has no friends.

Children find friends from all walks of life – just like anyone does – and home educated children are just the same. There is also a huge and growing community of home educators and organisations through which to contact them. There is always opportunity for interaction and support. No one home educates in isolation, unless they particularly choose to do so.

How parents and children get involved, plus other aspects of friendships, relationships and social development, is discussed in Chapter 4.

There are so many reasons we want to home educate it is hard to summarise them succinctly, but our main ones are as follows: we think that mass schooling has grown piecemeal as a response to adults' working patterns rather than according to children's needs and takes over a child's life with no time for hobbies, friends, dreaming or running around outside… Schools effectively insti- tutionalise children, leeching their responsibility away from them and teaching that learning is a chore… Children are taken out of society and isolated within large groups of their own ages, not learning how to fit into society or interact sensibly with people of all ages… Children at school don't learn useful life skills such as growing food, cooking, dealing with finances, how to amuse them- selves… We want to avoid harmful peer pressure until our children are old enough and secure enough to withstand it and not be pressurised into

> *unhealthy behaviour just to fit in… We feel that by home educating we will be offering our children a happier, healthier and more free childhood. In fact we will be offering them a real childhood instead of a race to grow up as quickly as possible and become exactly like everyone else.*
>
> **Parent, home educating two children since birth**

The disadvantages

Home educating is not without disadvantages. These vary from family to family and depend very much upon personal circumstances, a family's reasons for home educating in the first place, and the children's characteristics and learning preferences. However, the disadvantages are more to do with the parents' personal resources than they are to do with education.

The most obvious and probably the biggest disadvantage to deal with is to do with the parents' commitment, the sacrifice of their time and energy and the potential loss of an income. Also, as the children get older and move towards gaining qualifications, the management of study, resources and sitting exams becomes more complicated. However, these disadvantages can differ with families' personal points of view and perspective.

For example, some families who live in a very isolated location may feel that they need larger groups of children to interact with. Whereas other families, whose children may have experienced bullying, may feel that to have smaller, more intimate groups to interact with is an advantage.

For some families the possible loss of one income is a real and huge disadvantage, whereas others may see it as an opportunity to downsize and spend more time with their children.

Some parents would consider it extremely difficult to have to be with their children all day, whereas others would view it merely as an extension of what they already do as a parent.

Some parents would find the anxiety about their children's learning too much to overcome, whereas others who have children in school who are failing to learn would welcome the opportunity to have better control over their children's achievements.

Home education is a very personal decision and a very individual style of learning, therefore, exactly like the advantages, the disadvantages are different for everyone. However, the common belief among most home educators is that the disadvantages are outweighed by the benefits.

Many of the concerns that home educators have are the concerns that *every* family has, whether home educating or not. Some families have both children in school and children who are home educated. The only difference, they tell me, is that the school children tend to come home grumpy! No one seems to learn any more or less – they just learn differently. These families generally feel that for them the disadvantages of home educating are far fewer than the disadvantages they experienced with school and the disadvantages are far outweighed by the *benefits* to their child.

I feel that the disadvantages of home educating are far fewer than the disadvantages of school. It was not our original intention to home educate because we had not known about it, but it has been a very positive experience.

Parent of four children, two of whom have been through school and
two of whom have been home educated for the past seven years

There is one disadvantage that is common among all home educators though. One that all home educators find extremely unfair: there is absolutely no financial support for home education whatsoever. Not even with exams. This does not mean that home education is hugely expensive; it doesn't have to be. It is the examinations that incur the greatest cost. Some families overcome this by re-registering their children at a school at that time. But any families considering home educating need to be aware that they have to fund any external tutoring, courses and examinations themselves.

What do you need to home educate?

Most parents start home educating with nothing other than that which most parents would have, a *dedication* to the education and welfare of their children. This involves:

- *Commitment.* Home education is a huge commitment both of time and energy. You need to have the time to devote to it and the energy to get involved.

- *Rapport.* You need to have a good rapport with your children and enjoy being with them. Their education will essentially be based on communication between parent and child.

- *Dedication to learning.* You need to be able to encourage your children to learn, and to learn yourself. Home education is a learning journey for all the family, even though you need to learn different things.

- *Work.* You need to be able to manage your work around the commitment of time that home educating requires.

- *Somewhere to learn.* There needs to be a place in your house where children can work. Some home educators designate a whole 'school' room. Others have no particular room at all. They use the kitchen/dining room/bedroom table/corner/desk/floor as they would for homework or other activities, integrating the space within family life.

- *An interest in finding out.* You need to be able to source information. An encyclopaedic knowledge or personal qualifications are not necessary. No one has a knowledge of everything. No one is an expert in every subject. What's important is an interest in finding out what you and the child need to know and having the skills to do so.

- *A computer.* You need a computer or access to one. Computer literacy is part of a child's education. The Internet gives access to nearly all the information you need. It is also an integral part of the home educating network, keeping you in contact, essential if you live in an isolated location.

- *Integration.* You need to be able to get out and about either by car or public transport for educational purposes and social interaction.

- *Books and resources.* The amount of books and resources home educators have is entirely personal. It depends on the subjects studied and the approach each family adopts. There need not be a huge cost incurred. There are many home educators on very low incomes who manage with little extra expenditure than if their children were in school.

The above may seem daunting, but it is really nothing more than what one already does as a parent. It is perhaps more important to be adaptable, to have patience and tolerance, an open mind and a sense of humour!

Clearly, home education would not be suitable for everybody. But *anyone* can choose to home educate if they so wish. And everyone has the right to do so.

Summary of the main points

- Home education is a workable and legal option for parents who want to educate their children without sending them to school.

- Parents home educate using a variety of resources that exist within their community, using readily available schemes of work, the Internet, and by interacting with others.

- It is an approach that gives parents and children real options and enables them to choose which subjects, methods and approaches they use for their education.

- There are thousands of families already home educating and the community is growing all the time as increasing numbers of parents become unhappy with schools.

- It is an option open to any family whether they are teachers or not or whether they have any qualifications or not.

- It has many advantages, the most important of these being that it gives parents the opportunity to individually tailor the education of their child to suit their particular needs.

- It also enables children to learn in an environment where they are completely comfortable and where they will never have to suffer bullying.

- It is an opportunity for children to have a happy educational experience.

- The biggest disadvantage is the commitment of time and energy that is needed by the parent.

- The most important things you need to home educate are to be flexible and open minded, have patience and tolerance and a sense of humour.

Suggested websites

Education Otherwise: www.education-otherwise.org

Home Education UK: www.home-education.org.uk

Home Education Advisory Service: www.heas.org.uk

Chapter 2

How Do Parents Start Home Educating?

In this chapter we will look at:

Considerations when making the decision to home educate

The difference in deciding pre-school or after the children have been in school

The home education network and how to find support

Deregistering children from school

The role of the education authority

How home educators fulfil their obligations to the local authority

Making the adjustment from school to home education

Dealing with objections from others

Having confidence in your knowledge of your child

Considerations when making the decision to home educate

Home educating is a huge undertaking. Making the decision to do so is probably the biggest step any family takes. But making that decision is one of the hardest tasks; once that's over the more practical steps that follow are often less monumental.

Any decision-making is going to be greatly affected by the reasons you want to home educate in the first place and whether your children are of pre-school age, or are already in school. This is important and will be discussed shortly. First, though, there are considerations you'll need to think through that tend to fall into two categories:

- educational
- personal.

I list below some things to consider from both categories. They need thinking about, but that doesn't necessarily mean that you'll have all the answers to how you're going to home educate right from the start. No home educator does. It is very much something that families grow into and develop answers to as they experience it, just as they do with parenting. Home education is not specific; it is personal and as such variable. *Awareness* is more important at this stage than answers. Don't be daunted by the amount there is to think about – chew it over gradually.

It is also important to mention that some families, whose children may be really suffering in school, take the plunge to remove their children from school without making these considerations up front because their *immediate priority is the welfare of their child*. These families still go on to home educate successfully, coping with these issues afterwards, dealing with them as they arise. As with all decisions the child's needs are paramount.

EDUCATIONAL CONSIDERATIONS

- How interested are you and your family in education and learning? Your children will not be the only learners in the household. Home education affects what you as parents learn as well. It's not about an in depth knowledge of all subjects, nor insider knowledge of school methods, but rather being open to learning itself.

- Are you aware of what children learn in schools and the curriculum? You don't need to know the entire subject content, but you might want to know what the subjects are and why they are learnt. You can easily find this out.

- Can you manage the research? You will need to be able to research information about home education; about the subjects your child is studying, about furthering their education if they choose. The Internet has made this so much easier for home educators as most of the information is there. Therefore...

- Are you computer literate? Can you become so? – you can learn alongside your child.

- Think about what you want your child to achieve. Have you thought why you want them to achieve that? Have you discussed it with them? This will vary with the stage they're at. The following chapters in this book will help you.

- Think about what subjects your child might need and why, or what skills your child will find most valuable in their lives in the future beyond school.

- Have you ever thought about how people learn? For example, there are all sorts of ways to learn, not simply through schools and teachers. For instance, children learn how to use mobiles without either of those.

These educational considerations might seem off-putting. Remember, it isn't necessary to have a specific answer to everything. It is only necessary to be aware that these things will need thinking about.

Another point to remember is that although your immediate concerns may be educational, they are not as difficult to overcome as you might think. Even if you have only a little understanding of children's learning, or subjects or curriculum you can very easily find out by research, asking around or looking on the Internet.

What might be trickier to overcome is your personal management of home education. This probably takes more working out than anything educational!

PERSONAL CONSIDERATIONS

- Do you have the time? Either you or a partner, or possibly a close relative, is going to have to be there full-time for your children. This doesn't necessarily mean teaching them all day every day. It just means that for a good proportion of each day your child needs adult time to enable their home education. (Apart from the obvious fact that young children should never be left on their own.) You will have to manage this around working/earning/personal time.

- Do you personally have the inclination to do it? It is a drain on your personal energy, as most activities with children are, as any teacher will tell you.

- Can you cope with your kids being around you all the time? Many parents heave a sigh of relief when their children are out at school all day. Many loathe it and look forward to the school holidays when they get their kids back. How do you feel about it?

- Are there people near you who can help out with this? Every parent needs breaks from their children just as the children need breaks from their parents. Other relatives, friends and home educators with whom you can do a time swap can help with this.

- What is your relationship with your children like? In order to home educate there needs to be cooperation, understanding and respect between you. Parents often find that once released from school their relationships with their children improve. But there needs to be compromise and communication on both sides, and the ability to talk to one another.

- Are you a flexible, adaptable and resourceful person? You will need all these skills in order to home educate. Home education is more about what resources you have personally than educational resources.

- Are you also a good manager? You will need to be able to manage to integrate home education within your family and working life. This is probably something you already do naturally as a parent. But be aware that home education is as much about management as it is about learning!

- How will you feel about the uncertainty and risk of stepping out of the mainstream? Some home educators say that there was more uncertainty and risk leaving the education of their children to schools. However, it takes a strong person to maintain their beliefs when all others believe something different.

✳

Always keep your considerations within the context of what you believe is right for *your child*.

✳

There is a lot to think about. But don't let it overwhelm you. Answers will come. Some home educators have had children in such desperate situations in school they decide to go ahead and think it out afterwards.

It will help you if you think back to the time when you were about to have a baby. You'll remember that you might have known an awful lot about the birth. But once you had the baby you realised you knew very little about actually being a parent. Then you suddenly had an awful lot of questions but very few answers. However, you'll know a lot more by now. You've learned it through experience.

This is the approach you need to take when considering home education. You need to be realistic about your commitment. You need to keep focused on your reason for home educating and how the above considerations fit within them. After that you need to accept that some answers can only grow with your experience.

It also helps to remember that, just like with becoming a parent, nothing ever stays the same anyway. Children never stay the same. And whatever your considerations now, they are always going to change.

So making the decision to home educate probably needs to be based on the child's needs *now*, rather than what might happen long-term. Your child's needs now, and therefore your decision to home educate, will be dependent upon whether your child is pre-school, or is already at school.

The difference in deciding pre-school or after the children have been in school

Making the decision to home educate before children ever go to school is quite different from deciding to do so once they have started. This is because for those parents who decide to home educate after their children have been to school it is usually a second choice (unless they only became aware of the option after the children had started). Their decision is often as a result of issues with school and some parents are forced into it because those issues become too great for school to remain an option.

If you are thinking about home education with your pre-school child you will no doubt be making the decision based on:

- what your child's current needs are
- how you want to fulfil your children's needs
- how you will do this educationally, personally and socially
- how you can do this better than school
- your personal educational ideas and philosophies
- your lifestyle choices and philosophies

- your feelings about what schools provide, or not.

Home education at this stage can simply be an extension of parenting and family life, with the gradual introduction of more formalised learning as the child's needs grow. Therefore this decision is not based on schools' failings, as it often is for older children, but is rather a positive and proactive choice every parent is entitled to make.

If you are thinking about home education as an alternative to the education your child is already receiving in school, your decision will probably be based on the fact that it is unsatisfactory and you want to make changes. As well as education, this could equally be to do with the social interaction in school, the well-being of your child, their health, or other personal or learning issues. Therefore your priorities will be very different. Prioritising is important when considering home education.

For example, if your child is really suffering in school your priority may be to withdraw them from school before any more damage is done and think about the practicalities later, as some home educators do and go on successfully to educate their children. Desperation made them act and they thought out the answers later. This is particularly true for children who are being severely bullied.

So although there are many things to consider listed above, all considerations are *always* in the context of the effect school is having on your child. Your main considerations may be:

- Is my child thriving and enjoying their education?
- Is my child happy and well?
- Is my child safe?
- Are they achieving to their potential?
- What can I provide better than schools?
- What does my intuition tell me?

✳

Remember when decision-making: the welfare of your child is always the first priority.

✳

Your decision will be dependent on your child's current circumstances. You will need to look at what the alternatives are and weigh it up. In some cases home education has provided immense relief from intolerable circumstances that some children have had to endure in school.

Some parents have been able to discuss their decision to home educate with their child's school and keep communication open between them. Other schools are not so empathetic as they see state education and home education in conflict with one another. This is a great loss as any child's education works best as a partnership between school and parents, as government suggests it should be. In reality, many schools are not open to home education as an alternative and do not feel able to offer flexi-schooling, where the child can be home educated for some of the time and attend school some of the time, perhaps for particular subjects. But few parents manage to obtain this arrangement with schools. It is a legal option, but at the school's discretion.

It is also important to know that any decisions can be reversed and there is always choice. Some parents home educate for a short while and the children return to school when the problems have been sorted out. Some remove their children from school and they end up never going back as home education works well for them. Some families start home educating and find it is not for them and the children return to school. Some children never go to school from start to finish. Some children are home educated throughout their primary years and go into secondary schools. Some go into schools when they are thinking about taking qualifications. There are endless choices and always the option of change.

> *Our initial idea was to do it for one year...after one year the children were happy and making some progress, so we decided to go on for a further two years. Now we are beyond that and taking things as they come.*
>
> Parent of two children, home educating for three years

Always remember that any decisions can be reviewed, just as any child's education should be.

You do not need to make the decision alone. In fact, it is important to discuss it with others to maintain a broad overview. There are many other home educators you can talk to. You can find them through the many home education networks.

The home education network and how to find support

Many people feel isolated at the thought of home educating and leaving mainstream education. This is usually as a result of being unaware of the growing number of parents already home educating. But…

✳

There's a whole home educating community already in existence.

✳

Groups of home educators meet and plan activities together, socialise and develop networks of support. Finding these others is like finding a world that's been there all the time without you realising. The way to find them is through home educating organisations. Three are listed at the end of the first chapter. The next step you need to take is to join one and get in touch with others. They have websites full of ideas that help with the decision-making, available even if you are not yet a member. But the best help of all is to talk to others already doing it so you can ask your questions first hand.

Through these organisations you will find families just starting out, families who've been home educating a year or two, and families with teenagers who've been home educating for years. It gives immense support just knowing these people are out there. Knowing that there are other people who are doing something different from the mainstream makes you feel less isolated.

Sometimes it's not easy adopting a radically different lifestyle from friends and neighbours, and there will be moments of doubt about whether you are doing the right thing for your child. At such times the support of family, close friends and other home educators is vital, and it's a good idea to establish a support network at an early stage.

Parent of three children, home educating for ten years

To find immediate support follow these simple steps:

1. Type 'home education' or 'home schooling' into Google or use the addresses at the end of Chapter 1.

2. Explore the home education websites.

3. Join one of the organisations.

4.   Identify the contact in your area and ring them up for an informal chat.

5.   Ask if there's someone you can speak to about making the decision.

6.   Find out if there are any meetings in your area.

7.   To get a balanced view you may need to speak to several different people.

The biggest organisation is Education Otherwise. On their website you will find:

- all the legal details you need
- experiences of other home educators
- details of how to join and who to contact in your area
- details of helpful booklets and other literature you can order
- links to other useful websites
- other useful articles and information.

If you are planning to home educate the best support you can get is from those who understand. However well meaning and informed people are they cannot give you the support, or the accurate information, of those who have first-hand experience. Just like with parenting, those who've done it make it look so easy! However, unlike parenting, home education is still a very new field that many people are ignorant of – even many professionals. You need contact with those already home educating in order to gain realistic information. And as there are so many different approaches that families take you may need to speak to several different families to gradually build a balanced perspective.

When I embarked upon this journey all those years back, little did I know how successful and happy an encounter it would be. Home education for us has worked amazingly well and my son is a well-rounded individual with many friends. There were occasions of self-doubt on my part; that's only natural, I think. But that's where local Education Otherwise groups helped with support and encouragement.

Parent, home educating for ten years

Deregistering children from school

This is the very simple task of removing your child's name from a school. If your child's name is not on any school register there is no one you are required to inform. But most parents with young children have put their name down on the local school register to ensure their child a place. If your child is already at a school then they will be on the school's register.

You do not need either the school's or the education authority's permission to home educate. But if your child is on a register, and you have made the decision to withdraw your child from school, then you will need to inform the school and ask them to remove your child's name from that register. In other words, deregister them.

However, there are two exceptions to this. If your child attends a special school in England you do need permission from the education authority to withdraw them. If you live in Scotland you do need consent from the education authority whatever school your child attends. (Further information about this is available on the websites.) There are slight variations in Wales, so check the Welsh Assembly Guidelines or with your local authority.

The education authority is the government department, through local authorities, that is responsible for seeing that all children of school age receive a suitable, full-time education. They do this mostly by providing schools for children to attend. But they also have a responsibility to those children who are home educated. Although you do not legally need to inform your local authority it is courteous to do so. When the school deregisters your child they will pass that information on to their local authority anyway.

You can inform the school of your intention with a simple letter. It is your decision whether you speak to them in person or not. But you will still need to put it in writing. Your letter could say that you have made the decision to withdraw your child from their school and to take full responsibility for their education yourselves. Therefore you wish the school to remove your child's name from their register. There are sample letters available through the home education organisations and on the Education Otherwise website.

Once you have deregistered you have fulfilled your obligation to the school. The school will inform the local authority and they in turn will contact you.

The role of the local education authority

The local authority (LA) is responsible for the education of all children of school age. This is whether the children are in school or not. Mostly their energy is taken up with schools and the children there, but they are also responsible for home educated children and have officers appointed to the task.

This service is in place for the benefit of all children. However conscientious we might be as parents there are always going to be some individuals who neglect the education of their children. There are also those who would use home education as a mask for truancy. The LA has the job of seeing this does not happen and of supporting home educators.

However, due to the enormity of their workload, mostly concentrated within schools, there is in reality little concrete support from the LAs for home educators. This varies greatly from county to county and depends which authority you come under.

Your local authority will probably have a website. Some of them give reasonable advice to those families wishing to home educate, so it is worth checking them out.

Some authorities are more supportive and empathetic to the work of home educators than others. Some of them are poorly informed and find it difficult to remain flexible in their understanding of what some home educators are trying to do, seeing their remit only as trying to get children back to school. Therefore it is important that *you* are clear about what you are trying to do for your child's education, that you have thought it through carefully, and that you can demonstrate that to them.

This is all they want. They want to be reassured that you are going to pay attention to the education of your child. Most authorities want you to reassure them in a formalised, academic way and will send you a big form on which to write all your intentions down. These types of forms ask you for your intentions, your plans and schedules of work, timetables, subjects, curriculum, your qualifications and your facilities. But you are not actually legally required to fill these in.

These forms are very much for the convenience of the LA officers, most of whom are only familiar with a school type approach to education. Many home educators find LA forms inappropriate to the nature of their provision so take the initiative not to fill them in, as is their right. Instead they write a letter or a statement informing the LA of their intentions for the time being and that these will be reviewed.

The LA may also write or phone you and ask to visit you in your own home to discuss your child's education. They may also want an educational welfare officer to visit. This department is responsible for the general welfare of your child. Again, this service is there to protect all children.

When starting out this may seem very daunting, so you need to keep it all within the perspective of which it is intended, for the care and welfare of all children. Obviously the LA has a big responsibility for all these children. All they want to do is satisfy that responsibility for themselves. All you need to do is reassure them that you are making proper provision for your child. But you do not necessarily have to do this in the way the authority requests as long as you provide alternatives. There are several ways you can do this.

How home educators fulfil their obligations to the local authority

Most home educators demonstrate the provision they are making for the education of their children in one of the following ways:

- By having the LA visit them in their home. The children may be present or not.

- By sending statements or reports to the LA offices.

- By showing concrete evidence or samples of their children's work.

- By meeting the LA away from the home, with or without the children.

- By having their provision endorsed by a recognised third party.

- By several of these methods.

Some home educators find the easiest option is to allow the LA to visit them in their home for a discussion about their children's education with the children present and show them a few samples of their work or activities. Some home educators find this too much of a personal intrusion and do not wish their children to be subjected to any kind of interview so make other provision like written reports.

What is important is that you are aware of your right to refuse a visit as long as you are willing to make other provision. You also have the right to negotiate with the LA how you wish to demonstrate your educational provision. The LA has *no* right to insist on a visit, test your children in any way or make intimidating demands or threats as, sadly, a few home educators have experienced.

Most home educators find visits from the LA informal and enjoyable. It is good to chat to other adults involved in education, the children like showing off their stuff, and it helps to establish a good working relationship. This only goes wrong when the officers who visit are ill informed or unsupportive, or when families are made to feel that their provision is lacking, or feel that they need to do masses of concrete academic work that is not relevant to their curriculum or style of provision, just to have something to show.

This is why you need to have thought through your provision. You do not need to be 'qualified' yourself or have a specific 'school' room. You do not need to follow a specific curriculum or timetable, or use specific workbooks or schemes of work. But you *do* need to know what you *are* doing and be able to justify it with *why*.

Here are some questions you might like to think about in preparation for contact with the LA, to demonstrate that you have thought it out. Don't worry that you don't have the answers yet – there are no right or wrong answers anyway. This book is to help you think them through.

- Do you want to take some settling in time to adjust? You have a right to request this.

- Has your child had problems in school and do you want them to be discussed?

- What subjects will your child study? LAs like to know you are paying attention not only to subjects like numeracy, literacy and science, but also to a broader range of activities including physical activity. Equally, the subjects you study might simply be what the child chooses and therefore not pre-determined.

- How will they study them? You may have a very informal approach or a structured approach or something in between. (You will find ideas on this in the following chapters.)

- Where will your child work? You are not required to have a specific room although you may prefer to do so.

- How will you tackle reading? You may use reading schemes and approach it formally; you may prefer to snuggle on the settee with a book the child chooses. Again, you will need to demonstrate you have thought about it.

- Will you be using a timetable? This could be a school-type timetable, or simply a family schedule.

- What time will your child start and finish work? You are not obliged to stick to school times or set times.

- Will you be following a curriculum? Again, you are not obliged to.

- How would you like to provide evidence of your child's education?

- Will you be doing tests, exams or qualifications? You are not obliged to do any. You may feel you cannot tell at this stage.

- What are your immediate intentions or priorities? This may be the well-being of your child.

- Have you long-term intentions or priorities at this stage? (See discussion below about these remaining subject to change.)

- Are you qualified to teach? You don't need to be. Your experience as a parent and your knowledge of your child may be greater than some of the teachers in school!

- Do you belong to a home education organisation? LAs are usually keen that you are.

- How will your child socialise? Check out Chapter 4 on socialisation if you are worried about this.

You may feel that the questions you are asked by the LA are not appropriate to what you want to do. In which case say so – and go on to talk about what *is* appropriate.

It may help you to have another experienced home educator assist you in dealing with LA requests or to be present during visits in the beginning. This is another advantage of the support network.

It is important to maintain that your provision is under constant review and subject to change. This is an obvious necessity of education, often overlooked, but there are several reasons why this needs to be. First, children's needs change constantly. Second, no one can predict how things are going to work out. And third, you want to stay flexible and keep your options open, as any education should do in order to remain appropriate to the child, but you also do not want to commit yourself to any kind of deadline that may, after a while, not suit your child's rate of development. In other words, there need be no age limits on learning.

Whatever provision you make it is perfectly reasonable for you to explain that your family needs a period of adjustment time in which to settle and that you will be in contact with the LA about your provision in, for example, approximately six months' time.

Making the adjustment from school to home education

Most families require a 'settling in' period whilst they adjust to home educating. The majority of LAs are sympathetic to this requirement. This time for 'settling in' will vary between families and will depend on how you came to home educate. For example, if your child has only just reached school age but is continuing to stay at home full-time, you may only need to continue what you already do. If your child has been in school it is more of an adjustment. This is particularly true of children who are unwell or who have had bad experiences associated with their education. They will need special care and time to heal.

Apart from the needs of the children, the whole family will need some adjustment time. It is unrealistic to expect too much too soon, both in terms of education and personal management. It is no small change to switch from a school life to home educating. The worry about education, your children's friends, leaving mainstream and taking responsibility can be stressful. Most home educators experience this. Most adjust. Most go on to home educate successfully.

Here are some tips to get you through this adjustment period:

- Relax! This is the most important one. Education doesn't have to be stressful.

- Give yourself time to explore home education, find out what others do and learn what you can.

- Allow your child time. Work doesn't have to begin immediately or last from nine till four with concentrated focus. This is not how it realistically works in school.

- Get in contact with other home educators.

- Some children may need considerable time to get over their school experiences and to become wholly well and wholly themselves.

- If your child is used to going to school and a scheduled approach, to continue with this approach is often a good starting point. Be aware though, that something that may take a whole period in school in a class of 30 with disruptions, may only take ten minutes to achieve at home. Your child will have much more 'free' time that is as valuable as 'work' time. Relax about this!

- Remain flexible. Don't worry if your first approach is not working. Just change it. Home education is a process of trial and error, with constant changes.

- Keep your child's needs foremost and remind yourself why you're doing this.

- Discuss a way of home educating together with your child. Talk about what you think they should do. Talk about what they think they should do, and why.

- Explore some of the educational resource books and workbooks in the major bookshops. Don't be afraid to let your child choose.

- Progress gently rather than intently.

- Enjoy yourself! Education *is* enjoyable. It is as valuable to visit a museum and chat about the exhibits as it is to study a history book.

- Pay as much attention to your own personal organisation and well-being as to that of your child.

- Plan time for yourself, when your child is busy with something, as well as planning your child's time. Ask that your child respects this personal time, as you respect theirs, and does not disturb you. This is a good habit to develop from the outset.

- Remember, there's no rush to do it all straight away.

Education is a rich, stimulating, enjoyable experience. Did you know that? Does your child know that from their experiences in school?

We tend to have developed an attitude that activities have to be gruelling to be educational – if it is enjoyable then it can't be educational. This is not true at all, as many home educators discover. But it takes time to adopt a different attitude and to find a different way to make it so. This won't happen overnight so keep it light until you find your way. An afternoon in the park observing and discussing what you see can be as educational as studying species in a textbook.

Some home educators may have a laid back approach that they've developed through experience, which you may find too unstructured for you. Others may have a rigid structure that you find too restrictive. Stick to the ways you are comfortable working with for now and remain flexible.

The most important thing is your relationship with your child. So make sure you have fun. Schools can sometimes steal fun not only from education but also from the parent/child relationship and create conflict, e.g. 'Do your homework or no telly tonight!' To home educate successfully there needs to be a different type of negotiation, always from a positive perspective, e.g. 'Let's get this written work done now then we can go swimming this afternoon.' Keep your relationship sweet and be prepared to compromise. Allow the child to take the lead sometimes.

✱

Remember: progress never happens overnight.

It is the result of a series of steady and gradual steps made over a period of time.

✱

Dealing with objections from others

Most people respond to the choice to home educate with interest and admiration. However, to many, home educating is still a fairly unrecognised and alien way of educating your child. And how do people usually respond to aliens? Shock, horror and fear! People who are fearful can sometimes be quite unpleasant.

Home educators are exercising a choice that is open to all parents. And quite often they make that choice because they are extremely dissatisfied with schools. Many, many, many parents moan about schools but most are unprepared to instigate change. When they come into contact with people who do, like home educators, it threatens their position and this is what causes some people to be both objectionable and unpleasant.

Sadly, some parents experience this from other family members, which can make their decision to home educate really difficult. This is where becoming involved with the home educating community and learning from other home educating families can help enormously. It will help you keep faith with what you're doing and strengthen your position. It will give you support.

Most objections are made out of ignorance. This is why it is important that you have your ideas clearly thought out. This will enable you to answer people who may object to your decision to home educate. The usual objections are things like:

- Kids have to go to school in order to learn anything.

- Kids have to go to school to mix.

- You're depriving your child of a normal life.

- Kids need to get used to the hurly-burly of school in order to survive in real life.

- Kids need teachers to get an education.

- Kids need school discipline.

- Your kid will end up as a freak.

- They won't get any qualifications.

None of these objections are accurate or based in truth. You should learn why throughout the rest of the book and from the examples of other home educators. Understanding *why* will help you answer any questions you may have to deal with about your decision to home educate and cope with any opposition you may experience about that decision.

Meanwhile it may help you if you also understand that home education challenges much of what people always thought was true about children's learning. It challenges a huge, traditional institution. It makes parents look more closely at the education of their own children. So it is no small thing that you do when you home educate. It's a brave step that can make others feel threatened. But if no one ever made any brave steps there would be no progress. Thousands of families have already taken that brave step, made the decision to home educate and do so successfully. There's no reason why you can't if you're committed to your child's education, prepared to do the research and put the time in, so have confidence in your convictions about the education of your child – trust your intuition.

You will no doubt be making the decision to home educate your child because you care for their education and well-being above everything else – never forget that, or that school is not the answer to every child's needs. Home education is not necessarily the answer to every child's needs either. So each one of us needs to remain flexible and accepting, rather than confrontational, towards other people's choices whatever they are. Each one of us has the right to make individual choices.

Once, one of my friends at drama club asked me, 'Aren't you intelligent enough to go to school, then?' when she found out I was home educated. I said, 'It depends on your definition of intelligence.' 'Cor,' she said, 'you are intelligent!'

Sixteen-year-old student,
home educated for eight years, now at college

Finally:

✳

You are likely to be the one that knows your child best.

✳

That's what you need to have confidence in over and above everything else.

Having confidence in your knowledge of your child

As parents we do know a lot about our children, although many of us fail to give ourselves credit for that.

Many of us spend the first five years of our children's lives exclusively with them. After they start school we still spend about 50 per cent of their waking hours in charge of them. In doing so we learn a lot about them. We learn to understand them. And we are in a better position than anyone else to recognise what their needs are.

Teachers have learned how to teach. They've learned some child psychology. They've learned about institutionalised education. They have not learned about your individual child.

A PERSONAL STORY

There is no doubt in my mind that most parents know their child best. I doubted it at first, when I was a young arrogant teacher who thought she knew everything. But it didn't take me long to realise that there was far more to children's learning than just teaching classes of them. When you are teaching classes of them you can conveniently lose individuals. When you are answering the external demands that all teachers have put upon them you cannot possibly fulfil each specific need, even if you had time to recognise them. It wasn't until I was a parent that I realised that no teacher can hope to understand each child's specific need like a parent does.

✳

Parents know best.

✳

Unfortunately there are many professionals who don't acknowledge this. After all, we all like to think that we are the best at our own subject. And many parents have been made to feel that their expertise with their own child counts for nothing. Many of us tend to think, 'What do I know? I'm only a parent.'

47

Parents know lots. Parents who are interested in their children, who have been involved with their children, who have given their time to raising their children, have a far better insight into those children's needs than anyone. Even educational professionals.

Educational professionals, parenting gurus, child psychologists all know their field. They know more about their subject than others. This doesn't mean they automatically know what's best for your child. Neither do family, friends, other parents or other professionals. Parents know best. Have confidence in what you see to be happening. Don't underestimate your judgement. Most particularly, don't underestimate:

- the *understanding* you have developed through time with your child

- what your experience of *living* with them has told you

- what you've *observed*

- what your *child* is telling you

- your *intuition* about your child's needs

- *your* skill and insight into your child's needs as a parent

- *your gut feeling.*

Obviously other people and other professionals have good advice. They will know about things you don't. Their opinions are valid.

So are yours.

Talk to others. Listen to their advice. Get a broader overview. Then, put that advice within the context of what *you* know about your child.

Education is not an exact science. And every child is an individual with individual needs. Have confidence in what you know about your child's needs and what you think is right for their education. You do not have to make your *child fit* into what may be appropriate for other children and their education. The best way to fulfil your child's needs is to *make an education to fit them* – not the other way round.

✳

You're the parent.

You have an understanding that no one else can possibly have.

Trust your judgement.

✳

Summary of the main points

- When deciding to home educate you will need to consider how you will manage your lives as a family, as well as how you will manage the children's education.

- You need to prioritise your considerations and keep them within the context of your child's personal welfare and their individual educational needs.

- It is important to contact other home educators through the ever-growing network to find help in making the decision, further your understanding of home education and obtain ongoing support.

- In England you do not need permission to home educate. If your child is in school you need to inform the school of your decision so that your child can be deregistered.

- Home educators are required to provide evidence of their education to the local authority. Most do this by allowing a home visit or making written statements.

- It takes some time to adjust to a home educating lifestyle and most parents make this adjustment through trial and error.

- Some people may object to your decision to home educate so it is important to think through your priorities and find support to help you cope with this.

- Most parents have the ability to recognise their children's needs better than anyone. Parents need to have confidence in their intuition about their child's education.

Suggested websites

Directgov: www.direct.gov.uk (type 'home education' in 'search this site')

ParentsCentre: www.parentscentre.gov.uk (type in 'elective home education')

Parentzone Scotland: www.ltscotland.org/parentzone

Home education in the UK: www.home-ed.info (look at 'getting started')

Chapter 3

How Do Home Educated Children Learn?

This chapter is all about children's learning. It is long, but it's not complicated. It's quite simple really, because learning is quite simple, although schooling has complicated it. The chapter has three objectives:

1. To increase our understanding about learning in order to help our children learn.

2. To look at some of the approaches home educators use when tackling their children's learning.

3. To help choose an approach and consider other aspects of managing learning at home.

To reach these objectives this chapter is broken down into manageable subsections, each with a Top Tip from the section at the end:

Our traditional view of how children learn

A broader view of how children learn

What children need, both personally and environmentally, in order to learn

The most valuable learning aid: children's love of learning

How children learn without teaching

How children learn from everyday experiences

The learning value of play

The difference between skills and knowledge

Home educators' different approaches and styles

A tightly structured approach

An autonomous approach

An approach in between

How to choose an approach

The use of time

Motivation

Children having charge of their own learning

Opportunities within the community for learning

Our traditional view of how children learn

Most of us take children's learning for granted. We actually don't think about it much, relying upon schools to do our thinking for us. When you home educate you need to think about it lots! Most particularly you may find you need to question all the things you traditionally associated with children's learning.

Traditionally, we associate all children's learning with schools. We tend to have the view of education that it is something taught in schools, by trained professionals who know how to teach better than anyone else; they know what to teach and why to teach it. We accept what these professionals tell us, that they know best and that going to school to get an education is best.

We also tend to believe unquestioningly that in order to learn stuff children *need* to be taught by these professionals. They *need* enforced discipline in order to be taught it. They *need* an institution in which to be taught it. And that schools and the subjects taught there, resulting in qualifications, provide the type of education that every child must have or they will have no future. We also tend to measure everyone's *intelligence* by this type of qualifying education.

These are the traditional assumptions that most of us have about education and learning and most of us accept these commonly held views without ever needing to look outside them.

If we're honest most of us never look beyond our first assumptions that:

- children won't learn anything unless teachers teach them

- children won't get an education without school

- children won't learn anything without being forced

- children's learning starts when they enter school and ends when they leave, both daily and life-wise
- children need school for discipline
- the things children learn in school are the things they need to know
- teachers and schools know best about learning.

However, when you home educate you begin to examine these assumptions. You begin to ask: are they always true?

Home education is proving that actually these statements are *not* always true. But whether they are true or not an important point is that other things are also true. It is also true that:

✳

Children learn in a whole range of different ways,

not just the way they do it in school.

✳

They can learn in ways we might have never realised were learning opportunities, in other places outside of school. They can learn at times when we might least expect learning to be happening, without teachers and without enforced discipline. And caring parents can help them to do this as well as teachers can.

One of the advantages of home education is that you can use a broader approach to learning than the one adopted by schools. This gives you so many alternative opportunities to enable your children to learn in ways that might suit them better, but which may not be available in school.

Top Tip for thinking about how children learn:

Look at your children. Think of something they have learnt without being formally taught, without school, without being forced. How to talk is a good example! How to use a mobile phone is another. What else?

A broader view of how children learn

It is true that children learn in school because teachers teach them. What might surprise you is that it is also true that they can learn without school, without teachers teaching them, without being forced. We can see this from the example of children learning how to use a mobile phone. Children mostly learn how to operate mobile phones without school, without teachers, without being forced. The reality is that children are learning *all* the time, whoever they're with, wherever they are, whatever they're doing. As well as in schools with teachers, children can learn in other ways too. In fact, much of what children learn is learned before they ever even get to school, through their own investigation. As a parent you will have taught your child much before they even got to pre-school. Your child has already been learning, without you realising perhaps, before school was even thought about.

Your children will have learned how to walk, how to talk, the skills that enable them to eat, wash, wee in the right place at the right time. They've probably taught themselves to use all sorts of tools like knives and forks, and machines like the DVD player and the telly. Even as they grow children continue to learn all sorts of things that no one formally taught them. The best examples are probably complicated computer games and other technological gadgets like MP3 players, etc.

These are complicated skills that children are learning all the time, increasingly as they grow, but they had no curriculum, no key stages, no tests or specially trained teachers in order to learn them. They also learn a lot of information from watching the television and the Internet, without having any specific programme of study.

So, children can still learn without the things we assumed they needed, they can learn outside of schools, they can learn before the age of four and after the age of 18, without a programme or curriculum of learning, without writing lots of stuff down, without books being involved.

Obviously, the things children learn by themselves they are keen to learn, which is not the case with much of what they learn in schools. So motivation plays a part (more on that later). But the fact remains that children can learn without much of what we originally thought was needed for them to learn. Children can learn in conditions outside those first assumptions we made.

In actual fact, in order for children to learn there really only needs to be a few things present:

- a stimulus
- support and encouragement
- a comfortable learning environment
- the motivation to learn.

These are the things that are most important for children's learning. They are more important than schools, teaching, testing or enforced discipline.

They are not particularly simple things, when you think about them deeply and their implications; in fact they are quite tricky to maintain. But put these things in place and you could get children to learn anything. Take away the limitations of our first assumptions about needing schools and teachers and everything we associate with them and it becomes apparent that children can learn anywhere, at any time, with anyone. It can be that broad.

It is this broader view that most home educators adopt to facilitate their children's learning. As well as recognisable methods such as the gradual progression through a scheme of written workbooks, most home educators also use a broad range of opportunities within their daily lives, their daily activities, within their environments, within their communities, to support and broaden their learning.

For example, simply taking a child shopping can produce an opportunity for learning a wide range of subjects across the curriculum:

- maths (use of money, numeracy skills, percentages, capacity and volume, weights and measures, shapes, graphs and charts, etc.)

- English (reading the labels, writing lists, planning, discussions which broaden vocabulary, etc.)

- science (nutrition, foodstuffs and their contents, mixing and freezing and melting and changing substances, materials, etc.)

- geography (sources, industry, production of food, country of origin, location of shop, map-reading, etc.)

- history (how industry and production of food has changed, food shortages throughout our history, etc.)

- arts and crafts, design and technology (investigation of packaging design, graphics, construction of similar packaging, creating design, construction of models using junk materials, etc.).

The opportunities for learning are endless when you take away the limitations of our first assumptions about *when, where and how* children can learn. Learning need have no boundaries when you look at it from this perspective. Those boundaries that we normally associate with learning evolved for the convenience of the adults, and for the convenience of teaching large numbers of children all together in schools. The *learners* don't actually need them in order to learn. If you are home educating you don't necessarily need them either.

Home education is a unique journey for each family – in our case it has allowed our children the time and space to discover and develop their individual passions and interests. In many subjects learning from direct experience of the world is so much more effective than second-hand learning from books. Often our children grasp concepts incredibly quickly when they are able to interact with real examples.

Parent of three children, home educating for ten years

Top Tip on using broader opportunities to learn:

To help you understand how to use broader opportunities for your children to learn, pick an interest your child has. It could be something as seemingly non-academic as dinosaurs or dolls' houses. Think of three subjects on a curriculum (numeracy, literacy and science, for instance). Think of ways to practise skills related to these subjects through their interest. Maths could be measuring and size. Literacy could be descriptive or informative writing. Science could be study of environments or materials.

What children need, both personally and environmentally, in order to learn

Surprisingly, children actually need very little in order to learn what *they* want to know. What's more difficult is getting them to learn what *we* want them to know.

Whatever it is we want them to learn, one of the most essential conditions to learning it successfully is that the children are comfortable. And this means personally and emotionally comfortable more than their physical environment being comfortable, although this is important too.

Some children fail to achieve their learning potential in schools because they are not comfortable within that environment; they are ill at ease, and some are unhappy. As I said at the start happiness is important, not necessarily ecstatic happiness, but reasonable happiness. For in order to learn well they need to feel:

- safe; not threatened, ridiculed, bullied, ashamed or afraid
- not desperate for the toilet, overly anxious about what others think of them, frightened of being made to look a fool

- confident about who they are, what they think and what they can do
- happy enough to make mistakes, for some of the best learning comes of seeing the solution to a mistake and having a go
- comfortable and confident with the people they are working with, children and adults
- most of all, *respected* themselves.

These are the conditions in which children learn best, the best type of environment we could provide in order for children to learn, before we even start thinking about curriculum or anything else. For this environment makes children feel comfortable with learning and that's essential for their learning future. Home educating gives you the opportunity to take away much of what prevents children in schools from learning well.

When parents think about home educating, and what children need to learn, they tend to think about desks, 'school' rooms, teaching, books, discipline and silence. But these things are not as basically important to learning as confidence, comfort, security, encouragement, stimulation and respect. A child can sit at a desk with a book in school with a teacher making dire threats if there isn't silence and learn a lot less than if he was sitting in the garden reading with a caring and encouraging adult who was making the book look interesting!

A PERSONAL STORY

A classic example of this happened with our youngest. I always created what I thought was the best environment for her to learn: telly off, quiet atmosphere, no distractions, sitting up at the table, etc. But she was still very reluctant to sit down and write a story. One night, having gone to bed after a very tiring day mostly outdoors, she got up again and announced she was going to write a book. I didn't interfere, being too exhausted by this time to bother! So she sat in front of the programme I was watching, toys all round, on the floor, obviously very tired and started to write. She wrote a page in her little notebook, constantly asking me for spellings. She wrote more the next day, at breakfast, in the car, in a restaurant. In fact she wrote more than she'd ever done in her whole life in all the places I thought would be too distracting and not conducive to learning! It made me look at the use of desks, quiet and teachers in a new perspective. It also demonstrates that when the child is comfortable and confident, secure and feels encouraged they can learn just about anything. Provided they've got the motivation, of course.

To conclude, children can quite easily learn all the things they learn in school but without the school environment. They can learn equally well in a home environment. Many of them can learn better. Providing a good environment in which your children can learn is the starting point for getting them to learn well.

When thinking about providing a good home educating environment consider that:

- a good learning atmosphere, and this can be anything from a stimulating buzz with loud music to a studious murmur, is more important than silence

- basic needs, like having a wee, being fed, not anxious, frightened or worried about anything, or unwell, should first be met

- comfort is more important than uptight rigidity. Working on the floor or settee is as valid as working at a desk if it produces the same results

- praising even little achievements is more encouraging and therefore effective than berating what has not been achieved

- stimulation works better than bullying

- mistakes are learning opportunities not shaming opportunities

- mutual respect is paramount

- self-confidence is the best personal tool any learner can have.

It is so important that the learner feels comfortable. It is *their* needs that are the priority, not our traditional need to have hush, or have kids sat at desks, or shouted at for doing things wrong. Children can learn in all sorts of different environments and personal needs vary between children. Some children *need* to fiddle with something in their hands rather than sit still. Some need quiet, some need the buzz of others around. Some need solitude, some company.

When you are home educating you can look at providing for your child's individual needs rather than accepting the traditional view of what a learning environment should be like. It certainly does not have to be strict, restrictive or uncomfortable. Comfortable learners learn best.

> *My eldest son decided that he wanted to do his studying down where the family was, despite the distractions from two younger brothers, PlayStations, computers, pets and the general mayhem of family life. I wasn't sure this was the best climate in which to study but he went on to get A* in his results!*
>
> Parent of three children, home educating for ten years

Top Tip on learning environments:

Always create a comfortable learning environment and attitude to learning rather than a traditional or a harsh one. It will produce greater results.

The most valuable learning aid: children's love of learning

Home educating gives parents the opportunity to fully utilise the best asset to learning their child has: their inherent curiosity.

Curiosity is simply the desire to learn about something. Children are curious; they *love* learning. But most parents don't realise this. Or they don't believe it.

Think back to when your child was really little. What did they do? I bet they opened drawers, used your lipstick or shaver when you were not looking, pressed switches, poked the pets, rummaged in the dustbin, tasted the beetle crawling across the floor, snipped bits off things, probably their hair!

Did you ever stop to think about why they did these things?

Most of us assumed that our children did these things to be naughty, to wind us up, to get our attention, to make themselves as irritating as possible! But those assumptions are wrong. Children do these things usually because of their curiosity, their burning desire to find out. In other words, to learn about something. To learn what happened if they poked the pets, what was inside the drawer, how things worked, etc. It was all about learning. That's how small children begin to learn about their world and practise the skills needed to operate within it.

And they simply love doing that. Small children are simply a little bundle of eagerness to learn. In fact they're desperate, so desperate sometimes that the frustration they feel when they are prevented, as we so often do by shouting 'put that down', 'leave that alone', 'no you can't' etc., produces a tantrum.

This desire to learn will make children take all kinds of risks to find out what happens. Like throwing themselves in the deep end at the swimming pool when they can't swim, as my youngest did. Like seeing how high they can get up a tree. Or touching something hot to see what it feels like. Kids want to know things. They are born wanting to learn. Although you wouldn't know that by the time they get to secondary school!

So what happens to that desire?

This is the question that started us out on the road to home education. I saw all the eager little toddlers so keen to learn about everything that adults knew about, asking their endless 'why' questions. At the other end of the spectrum I saw disenchanted teenagers standing about the town precincts not interested in anything. And I thought, what happened to their love of learning? Where did it go?

Those teenagers are not standing around there doing nothing because they don't have a brain, as some adults would like to think. It's just that their love of learning, of living a learning life as we all actually do all of the time, has been extinguished. They have little motivation any more.

In actual fact, we all love to learn (when the motivation is there of course). We learn for promotion and to better ourselves, to drive a new car, to use the new media centre, bits of a foreign language when we're on holiday, to visit new places. We upgrade our skills all the time. We are motivated to learn new things throughout our lives. And children most particularly are because for them everything is new and worth investigation. They're fascinated.

That fascination and interest in their new world is the best form of motivation; it is the best aid home educators have at their disposal to facilitate continued learning. If kept alive it can be used to motivate children's learning across all subjects, across all ages. Unless their desire to learn is destroyed.

It can be destroyed through the child being made to feel uncomfortable about learning or with the environment in which they learn. It can also be destroyed through teaching.

Teaching can be inspirational. It can also be destructive. The next section discusses it.

Top Tip on children's love of learning:

Think about your child's curiosity. Listen when they ask 'why'. Nurture their interest in everything. Respond to their questions. Allow them to investigate. Encourage them to explore (safely). Keep their love of learning alive. It's the best asset children can have for their education.

How children learn without teaching

Most adults still hold the view that children need teachers to learn. However, we can see from the ways in which toddlers learn that it is possible to learn many things without teachers and without being taught.

This can also be true of academic study. Anyone who has ever done any kind of home study course, or learned the driving theory, will know that it is possible to learn without teaching. Most of us learned our driving theory without any kind of teaching. Most children learn how to text, use MSN or computer game networks without being formally taught.

Children learn these things without teaching by:

- trial and error
- first-hand experience
- exploration and explorative play
- investigation and investigative play
- physical practice
- being comfortable and confident enough to have a go.

Put any new toy or gadget in front of a child and these are the methods they will employ in order to learn how to use it. They certainly can't leave it alone. Sometimes they'll ask for help. Mostly they want to do it for themselves.

This desire to learn for themselves, and the methods they use to do so, can be equally successful as being taught by someone else. In fact, it is often more successful because teaching can sometimes intrude upon a child's learning; it can switch off a child's desire to learn, and at its worst it can make a learner feel uncomfortable and unhappy.

This can happen with careless teaching, when a teacher has a lack of respect for the fact that a child can and might want to learn something independently, when a teacher makes the learner feel inadequate or inferior, when the methods teachers use make the subject dull and uninteresting. Unfortunately this can so easily happen within a school framework, where overstretched teachers have to deliver a curriculum to large numbers of children in a small space of time and therefore don't have the time for individual requests, investigation and practical application. Neither do they have much time to tend to individual learning needs.

Although it is a method that we may not normally associate with education, many learners learn far better when allowed to learn for themselves than when taught by someone else who has control over the situation. Learning independently gives the learner control, makes them feel valued and that their learning has purpose. It's a fantastic life skill. It keeps their love of learning alive and therefore keeps them motivated. Teaching can so easily destroy all those things.

Originally teachers were needed because most people didn't have the knowledge or the information teachers had. Due to the Internet, that has all changed. Everyone now has access to information. Children have the opportunity to find out for themselves, rather than be taught, more than they ever did.

Home education gives parents a greater opportunity to allow the child to use their own methods of learning, as well as perhaps being taught sometimes. Self-learning removes much of the danger of a child having their love of learning destroyed by poor or intrusive teaching.

The trend in schools is moving towards this very concept of giving children more responsibility for their learning. This is one of the major reasons for homework. Homework is intended to provide the child with opportunities to take charge of their own learning rather than have it always taught to them by a teacher, or enforced.

Unfortunately, most children don't want to do a night's homework after a whole day at school, and who can blame them! The other problem is that after years in school being taught, children really have no idea *how* to be responsible for their own learning because their learning has always been taken over by someone who professes to know better. And by this time children may have had their love of learning dulled by the methods used – sometimes methods as abhorrent as ridicule and shame – and the subjects covered in schools, so they have no motivation to do it. So homework doesn't work particularly well for them in that respect.

After three years of trying different routines, I've found that there has been no one-way. It's seasonal, it's developmental and children change their minds! Routine for us is when there are days in and days out; work on a theme for a week and coast along for two! Being a role model, a facilitator, carer and dinner lady. Rarely a teacher!

Parent of two children, home educating for three years

However, home education is like doing your homework in the day, and it can work brilliantly if the children are encouraged to be in charge of their own learning and find out (research) for themselves, rather than always relying on being taught. Most home educators, therefore, tend to see their role more as a facilitator to their children's education, constantly guiding and encouraging, rather than actually teaching. Many children learn well by this approach.

It takes a while to develop an approach where children are encouraged to learn for themselves rather than always being taught. The way to encourage it is to always involve your children in decision-making about what, where, how, and why they have something to learn (more on this in the section about children taking charge of their own learning).

Children who are learning without teaching, learning by themselves, also have the best opportunity to discover things through their own experiences. And first-hand experience can result in the most meaningful learning, and is the learning that is retained the best.

The next section looks at ways to learn through first-hand, everyday experience.

Top Tip on how children learn without teaching:

Rather than worrying that you need to be a teacher, see your role as a mentor and facilitator of your child's education. Lay out opportunities, and encourage the children to learn for themselves, e.g. you don't need to 'teach' measurements in metres and centimetres. Give the child a tape measure, explain the units and encourage them to go off and find five things a metre long, five things 10 cm long, measure the kitchen table, etc. Even more fun with a long tape outdoors.

How children learn from everyday experiences

Having first-hand experience of something is the most effective way of learning. By first-hand experience we mean actually physically experiencing something, rather than being told about something. Being told about something comes from someone else; it is second hand.

The Top Tip at the end of the previous section is an example. Being told about metres is second-hand learning. Having a metre stick in your hand and seeing the units, going around and practising using it, getting the 'feel' of a metre and applying the use of your understanding is gaining first-hand experience. First-hand experiential learning stays with the learner the best.

If you look back over your own learning it is probably the first-hand experiences that taught you the most and that meant the most to you. For example, seeing Shakespeare performed on the stage, or as a film, brought it home much better than by simply reading the play and have a teacher talk about it. It got you more involved, it gave you visual stimuli by which to remember it. And it was a lot more fun. Learning that is fun is usually remembered.

There are lots of opportunities in our everyday lives to relate children's learning to first-hand experience. This is a method of learning that many home educators use to facilitate their children's learning and support academic study.

Whatever curriculum or content of learning you follow much of it can be learned from first-hand experience. Unfortunately schools and teachers have little opportunity to take full advantage of this. But home educators have as much opportunity as they wish to make their children's learning first-hand or experiential, rather than always delivering it second-hand through text and workbooks.

Here are some examples of ways in which you could turn second-hand learning into first-hand experiences:

- Rather than studying the concept of capacity in a workbook get out as many containers as you can find and measuring jugs, give them to the children and allow them to find out how much things hold, what a litre looks like, or millilitre in a similar way to using the tape measure in the previous Top Tip.

- As well as doing sums get out as many different materials to count as you can find: Lego bricks, soldiers, dolls' shoes, pasta, raisins, cutlery, anything, and practise the four rules of number – adding, subtracting, dividing and multiplying – by physically counting and grouping.

- Rather than merely studying a diagram naming the parts of a flower, get real flowers and allow the child to dissect them and discover the real parts for themselves, using the diagram to name them.

- To reinforce reading about the war get off to a museum that has displays, or an airfield, or a re-enactment, and discuss everything you see.

- Nearly everything that is covered within a basic science curriculum can include some real practical experiences for the child, even if it is simply going for a walk and identifying species or looking for materials, or physically mixing substances.

- Get a newspaper or magazine and look at it together, identifying all the different writing strategies employed there: informative writing, persuasive writing, etc. rather than just sticking to a scheme workbook.

- Use galleries, exhibitions, displays, workshops and museums as much as you can.

- Don't underestimate the powerful learning potential of chatting about these experiences as they are happening. Discussion is an opportunity to cement understanding and build memory triggers.

If you keep thinking about providing first-hand experiences for your child in this way, rather than sticking to second-hand study all the time, you will help to keep your child interested, responsive, and their love of learning alive. Home education gives you the opportunity to do this much more than is possible in school. An immense amount of learning just naturally happens through these first-hand experiences and it is retained more effectively than through any other method because it is visually and physically stimulating.

Some parents might worry that their children were not learning because these first-hand learning experiences do not necessarily provide written proof that learning has been taking place. Children in schools have lots of books with things written in them. They have lots of worksheets with ticks on them. They have masses of paper evidence of what they've done in school. However, this doesn't necessarily *prove* that a concept has been *learned*. So many children dutifully write down all the notes that they are expected to have learned, but have very little *understanding* of what it's all about.

Practical experiences help to cement understanding. Learning is about understanding, not necessarily about having lots of written work. Understanding is the basis on which formalised written work can then be built.

In schools much of children's work is done second-hand through reading and writing. Reading and writing is not always the most effective way of learning. In fact, it is impossible for some children to learn in this way. Intelligent children can appear to be failures in school because most learning is based on reading and writing, yet their intelligence is clear when you talk with them. For these children, and for many others, learning through first-hand experiences and discussion is a method that brings success.

Don't underestimate how much your children are learning through these first-hand experiences even though they're not producing written work about it. Concentrate on the learning *experience and understanding*, rather than how much written work is being done. Written work keeps children in school busy and produces proof of subjects covered to parents. Home education does not require either of those outcomes.

Some of the best opportunities to incorporate first-hand learning experiences into children's learning come through play. The next section discusses how.

Top Tip on learning from everyday experiences:

Cooking is a great way to learn from first-hand experience. The subjects it covers are: substances and their changing states, heating and cooling and the use of related materials, nutrition and health, weighing and measuring and reading off scales, various hand/eye coordination skills, reading and interpreting a recipe and instructions, time and temperature, and if it all goes wrong: problem solving!

The learning value of play

It is easy to get hung up about play, about the fact your children are spending time 'playing' rather than 'working'. Parents see their children 'playing' with water or with the tape measure or the weighing scales and feel anxious that they should be 'working'. This is particularly true when it happens in school and the young children come home and say they've been playing with the sand or in the Wendy House and parents think the children should be getting on with 'work'.

What is often misunderstood and underestimated here is the huge learning potential of this type of play. This kind of play gives the children opportunity for first-hand experience, it stimulates all kinds of brain functions as well as their imaginations, it increases their understanding, it cements that understanding, it helps them retain learning, it helps them apply their knowledge in practical situations, it develops all sorts of skills. Play stimulates children's intellectual and social and emotional development enormously.

Swimming is an example of how a child can learn through play. If you continued to give your child the opportunity simply to play in a pool they would no doubt end up being able to swim. It might be a clumsy style. But that could soon be tidied up easily with more formal lessons, for much of the basic concept of swimming would already have been learned: confidence in the water; buoyancy; how their body resists or moves through water; how different movements aid those processes, etc.

Playing with water will have far more impact on a child's concept of capacity than ticking multiple-choice answers in a workbook, for example. Working from workbooks gives us full workbooks. But could a child estimate or recognise a litre of water? Do you know how long a kilometre is – have you actually walked it?

Nothing reinforces a concept more soundly than having experienced it. Through play, children can experience such a wide range of concepts. And this is the case across the curriculum. There are all sorts of ways children can 'play' for this purpose. For example, taking three important subjects:

- maths: play with real money, play shops, play with things they can group and sort and count, constructional toys, play with shapes, play with containers and a variety of substances to fill them, not just water, e.g. lentils, flour, beans, cornflour and water, rice, etc., using facilities to weigh and measure a variety of units, playing with a stop watch...

- science: play with a variety of substances from your store cupboard, inventing potions and drinks, freezing and heating them; play with materials (indoors and out) like sand, bricks, wood, stones, sticks, leaves; play with the variety of science kits available, exploring for natural things, making collections and classifying them; play 'dens' in as many different environments as you can visit (indoors and out)...

- English: children always seem to love playing at writing, making books, playing with books, making up stories (spoken are as valid as written); playing at phoning each other up, playacting or drama that involves speaking, inventing words; playing on the computer, or with magazines and comics give as much potential for practising reading skills as books do; colouring-in and similar activity books greatly help hand-eye coordination and manipulative skills needed for writing...

Play is merely first-hand practical learning. While children are playing they are stimulating their imaginations, they are investigating, they are experimenting, they are finding out, their brains are working in numerous ways.

Play of this nature gives a strong foundation for so much of what children are required to know in schools and it can continue across the curriculum.

Even older children can learn through this type of play, although their play becomes more sophisticated. Exploring the Internet for information, for example, using the computer – much of their learning can be done through computer programmes, using more complicated tools, machines and gadgets; building or constructing with any materials, designing, experimenting with as many different art materials as they can, not forgetting that cloth, wood, metal, scrap materials and other mediums (even dead animals in the case of Damien Hirst) have all been used for great artworks; they can play with recipes and more sophisticated substances. Many a great discovery was made through this type of play, by experimentation and investigation.

In fact, it is exactly this type of activity that child psychologists and parenting gurus are now saying that we need to be encouraging our children to do. They say our children should be playing more. This type of learning keeps children motivated. It is the foundation on which they can easily build their knowledge and skills for their more academic learning.

It doesn't matter how long they want to do it, how often, how strange, or how old the person is. Carl Jung the famous psychiatrist is reputed to have made mud pies even as an adult because it helped him to think! If you think about it, we all do still play. We play with our new cars, our new gadgets, our new outfits, trying them out, exploring what they do. This is how we get to grips with them, learn about them. Children need to do that with all the things they come across in their world in order to learn and create a foundation for the more academic parts of their education.

Children playing are *actively* engaged. And this means active mentally as much as active physically, and this is important for learning. They are usually moving, fiddling with their hands, arranging, manipulating tools, toys or materials and they are usually chatting either to others or themselves; their whole being is focused and they are engaged and absorbed in the activity. They are interacting. When children are watching the telly, for example, you can usually see that they are passive, they are not responding, they are glazed. This state is less receptive to learning.

✳

Play stimulates the brain. A stimulated brain is a learning brain.

✳

Stimulating the brain is essential for learning. While the child is engaged in this way much learning occurs *incidentally*. Incidental learning is as valuable as learning that has been planned towards a specific outcome.

A PERSONAL STORY

I was very relieved the day I read about Carl Jung and the mud pies because my youngest spent hours doing just that. She too said that it enabled her to think. However, as she's got older, she's turned to pottery and produced some exquisite jugs and bowls! My eldest spent time playing at wrapping bits of rag and cloth round her dolls. She now makes herself stunning outfits.

Home educating gives you the opportunity to use the potential learning power of play. Don't waste it. And never underestimate its influence on your child's learning.

Top Tip on the learning value of play:

Don't be afraid to allow your children to play. Give them as many different objects, materials, tools and substances to play with as you can. And think beyond the norm – we gave ours anything that we'd finished with (DVD player, old mobile, clothes, Hoover) to play with or dismantle. Give them different environments to play in. Give them different people to play with and a variety of opportunities for play outside the home as well as in.

The difference between skills and knowledge

As a final section on increasing our understanding of learning before we go on to learn about different approaches home educators use, it might be helpful to look at the difference between skills and knowledge. We all know what knowledge and skills are. But what we fail to understand sometimes is the fact that one is pretty useless without the other. They need to be in balance.

I mention this because it is one of the areas where the education children receive in school has become out of balance. During recent years the education of our children in schools has been very much knowledge based. Schools have been focused on filling children's heads with facts. What has now been realised is that this has produced young people who may have knowledge of a subject, but have very few of the skills needed to *apply* it. Without those it is little more than useless. So the move now is towards making learning in schools more skills based.

Much of the type of learning I have outlined above has emphasised the use of practical, first-hand experiences, encouraging children to play, experiment and investigate in order to learn. This type of learning is where children gain *skills* as well as understanding. Not only physical skills like use of tools, for example, but mental skills, like being able to judge exactly how long a metre is, or what the feel of a kilogram of flour is like, or how to tackle something if it goes wrong: vital thinking skills that help them apply their knowledge to living.

Problem solving is often included in a curriculum in school. Ironically, problem solving is something everyone does, every day, in the course of living a life. Tackling it only in a school situation will do little to equip children to cope with problems as they come up in everyday life outside school. Many of them faced with not being able to do something give up because they haven't got the skills required for lateral thinking. Lateral thinking is being able to think things out from all angles. Children are so often stumped when their first attempt goes awry because they are drilled to think in a set pattern, to produce one answer, usually out of a choice of answers, rather than from scratch. Thinking is just another skill often neglected.

Experiential learning, practical learning involving lots of activity and investigation and learning through play all help to develop valuable thinking and other skills that make knowledge transferable to real life.

For example, it's no good being able to do percentages in a book if you've no idea what it means on your savings account or when you're shopping in the sales. It's not a lot of good recognising nouns, adverbs, adjectives and complicated linguistic devices if you haven't got the skills to write a good CV or personal statement. The study of nutrition in schools is the best example. Children learn all about balanced diets, what food groups are essential for good health, and what foods contain these essentials. However, many children seem totally unable to see how this applies directly to them, to their lifestyle, to their health, fitness and overall happiness.

Knowledge is, of course, essential. But it is fairly useless if you haven't got the skills to *apply* it. It is skill that enables the learner to use his knowledge for real living, not just for school. Many employers complain that young adults have lots of qualifications, but little ability to apply their knowledge to the workplace. This is due to lack of skills.

Home educators have the opportunity to readdress this imbalance. Giving children time to play, time to investigate, explore and discuss, and using a broad variety of learning opportunities alongside an academic curriculum, will give the children opportunities to learn valuable skills rather than simply filling their heads full of facts that seem unrelated to them and the lives they lead. Learning skills also gives a concrete practical basis for more sophisticated knowledge to be built upon. To have a valuable education children need a balance of both knowledge and skills.

In these information rich days it is our belief that acquiring a set body of knowledge is less important than developing flexible individuals with a good repertoire of learning, emotional and social skills. The skills that we seek to develop include:

- observation – this is considered fundamental as it underpins all other academic and life skills

- questioning – the ability to frame suitable questions is a key skill in all areas of life

- research skills – including gathering raw data, reading intelligently, use of information books and technology such as the Internet

- analytical skills – including use of logic, inference and deduction

- creative skills – we encourage this through art, craft, development of the imagination, role play and seeking creative solutions to life's problems

- presentational skills – including producing written work, graphs and diagrams, art or craft work and musical compositions

- physical skills – improving motor skills and coordination through activities such as swimming and climbing, cooking, art and craft and computer games

- emotional skills – including both intrapersonal and interpersonal skills, and most importantly developing a strong sense of humour to provide stability through the ups and downs of life.

Despite the emphasis on acquisition of skills, all our children have a wide range of general knowledge, which they have acquired naturally through exposure to a rich range of learning experiences and resources.

Parent of three children, home educating for ten years

> **Top Tip on practising skills:**
>
> Always try to give your child practical opportunities to use their learning and therefore practise their skills. For example, understanding fractions is very useful when you're cutting up the pizza. MSN and texting practise use of language as well as writing.

Home educators' different approaches and styles

Some of the ideas in the preceding sections of this chapter may appear to be very broad. They may suggest an unstructured approach to learning. In fact this need not be the case at all. They are ideas that anyone home educating can implement in a variety of different approaches to their children's learning. They could be incorporated into a structured approach where learning is tackled within a definite framework often guided by scheme workbooks, with timetables and specific learning objectives. Or equally into a child-centred, autonomous approach where learning outcomes are the direct result of the child's needs at the time. Or it may be that what suits best is a combination of the two. The next few sections look at these approaches.

A tightly structured approach

Some home educators use a very tightly structured approach to their children's learning. Their days are timetabled like a school day. They have a specific area or room for work. They use graded workbooks that take the learner through a series of academic exercises towards a particular learning outcome, workbooks based upon the National Curriculum. They choose subjects that children would be studying in school. They use academic tests and attainment exercises to judge their children's learning progress. This is very much a school-at-home approach which many parents find comfortingly familiar, probably having been to school themselves. They start with a specific curriculum, with specific timetables in which to implement it, and fit the child's needs within that framework.

Using a tried and tested approach like this can give confidence to any parent wishing to home educate. The curriculum is already set and requires little thinking out on the part of the parent. The workbooks and materials are fairly easily available in bookshops and online. Parents can be reassured that their children are receiving the same learning and structure of knowledge as children within schools. Adopting this structured approach can sometimes encourage children to settle to a working routine.

Advantages	Disadvantages
1. The pre-set curriculum usually has clear objectives so parents know exactly what subjects and curriculum content is going to be covered.	1. This approach is centred on a tight structure and curriculum rather than the individual.
2. This approach keeps children's learning on a parallel with children in schools.	2. Therefore individual learning needs can be overlooked.
3. It can make planning of your home education much easier, both in terms of your time and thinking up activities.	3. It offers little opportunity to take advantage of practical, experiential and incidental learning as it can lack flexibility, imposing time and content limitations.
4. Some parents find security in following an approach that everyone is familiar with and having their children's learning clearly mapped out.	4. Some children can become resistant and lack the motivation to learn in this way, especially those whom it doesn't suit.

Top Tip for a tightly structured approach:

If you are a person who enjoys a clearly organised structure in your day or are just starting to home educate, this is an approach you may find useful.

An autonomous approach

This is an approach which focuses entirely on the child. It starts with their interests and relates their learning specifically to their needs.

This means that whatever the child is interested in at the time they are allowed to pursue there and then, and learning opportunities revolve around that particular interest. The subjects covered, the pace at which they learn, arise from that interest. With an autonomous approach children generally do not pursue subjects or do research or academic practice simply because those subjects or activities are on a curriculum or timetable. The children do activities which they have chosen, when they have chosen them. Learning opportunities arise from the child's activities. Knowledge and skills result from following these interests and activities. If there is any sort of structure, timetable or curriculum it will be devised by, or in consultation with, the child, as are any methods adopted to facilitate learning.

This approach may to some lack the elements we commonly associate with children's learning. However, some home educators find it works extremely well as it entirely fulfils the specific needs of their children, needs that may not fit well within a tightly structured approach.

Advantages	Disadvantages
1. It fits learning round the individual needs of the child rather than the need to follow a curriculum.	1. This approach may require more thinking out from the parents.
2. It makes best use of the opportunity for incidental learning.	2. It does not have predetermined learning outcomes which some parents find disconcerting.
3. It removes time, place and content limitations and has great flexibility.	3. It is more difficult for adults to keep track of the child's learning progress.
4. It utilises a broad approach to learning which helps to keep children's love of learning alive and therefore keeps them motivated.	4. It takes more confidence to work with an approach that is less structured and familiar.

Top Tip for an autonomous approach:

This approach has great flexibility and suits many children who have difficulties with a school-type routine, academic activities and curriculum, or who learn better with a more practical, experiential approach.

An approach in between

The two approaches described above are extremes. They come at the ends of a spectrum of approaches which combine the two. Most home educators fall somewhere in between these approaches, using elements that work for them from both approaches and disregarding what doesn't. Their approach may change over a period of time in line with their children's learning needs and family circumstances.

For example, some families may adopt a formal and structured learning approach if this is what their children have been used to in school, then gradually move away from this to a more flexible approach as children discover particular interests and want to arrange their time differently to develop particular strengths.

Some home educators who may have adopted an autonomous approach whilst their children were younger begin to introduce more structure as the children want to reach specific academic goals, GCSEs for example.

Some families vary their approaches depending on the subject. For example, they may choose a structured approach to their child learning maths using a graded workbook and set times, but with reading might allow the child to choose what and when to read. Or they may choose a structured curriculum workbook but allow the child to choose which page to do first. Or follow a GCSE course but allow the student the freedom to choose when and where they study as long as they fit in, say, two hours a day. This gives families opportunities to change and be flexible.

The advantage of choosing an approach somewhere in between is the flexibility. It means that the approach you choose can be suited exactly to your child's needs. It can incorporate the best of both, yet disregard aspects that you find don't work particularly well for you. Flexibility makes best use of spontaneous learning opportunities as they arise. It also tends to suit family life the best.

We followed a fairly structured way of educating our son, using workbooks by Letts, WH Smiths, CGP and Carol Vorderman. He did his SATs tests usually two years earlier than he would have done at school. He did his 11+ aged nine, purely so we could see how he was doing compared to his schooled peers. We never did set hours or days; if it was sunny outside then we made the most of it. When his school peers were sitting at a desk in school we would be out enjoying whatever interested him.

Parent, home educating for ten years

For us, home education works best when it is an integral part of life. We have no set hours and our learning plans are flexible – the most effective learning nearly always takes place when we are relaxed and happy and often not actually doing anything specifically 'educational'.

Parent of three children, home educating for ten years

> **Top Tip for an approach in between:**
>
> Using the best of both approaches is more likely to keep you in tune with your child's needs than working rigidly to one approach or another.

How to choose an approach

It's important to realise that when home educating the approach you choose is entirely personal. And simple though it might be, no one can tell you exactly how you should be doing it. It also helps to recognise that possibly no one single approach will offer you the entire solution to your child's learning needs. And there is nothing anywhere to say that home educators should adopt a recognisable approach and stick with it for all their home educating days. No one would expect you to do this, not even the education authority. What is important is to:

✳

Do what works for your child and your circumstances.

✳

Here are some things to consider when you are choosing an approach to home educating:

- *The child's needs.* How do they learn best? Keep focused on that.

- *Your needs.* What do you feel confident with?

- *Your circumstances,* both practical in terms of the facilities you have in your house, rooms, etc. and personal in terms of your time and work.

- *Your child's circumstances*: this may depend on whether you have come to home education after difficulties in school and therefore they need a different approach to that right now.

- *You don't have to start out with a specific approach,* but can work day to day until you find a pattern or what works for you.

- *Flexibility.* Whatever you start out with does not have to remain forever. Your child's needs change so your approach may need to change.

- *Talk to as many other home educators as you can* about the approach they take.

- *If you adopt a structured approach* don't be afraid to take advantage of spontaneous opportunities for learning as they arise.

- *If you adopt a more autonomous approach* don't be afraid to introduce elements of structure to achieve specific goals.

- *Keep in mind the ways in which children can learn* as outlined earlier in this chapter and don't be afraid to try something that is new to you even if it isn't familiar.

- *Different subjects can suit different approaches.* Don't be afraid to switch between approaches, suiting the approach to the subject.

- *Trial and error will be the way to find what suits.*

Top Tip on using an approach:

It might be best not to worry about an approach but concentrate instead on understanding the myriad ways in which children can learn and developing the ways in which your child learns best.

The use of time

Most adults seem to get hung up with the concept of time. Most adults always seem to be running out of it!

We have all also been conditioned to think that there is a time limit on education, when actually there doesn't have to be.

Starting-out home educating parents tend to assume that they need to keep their children 'working' from nine in the morning till three in the afternoon. But this would be very difficult to achieve and perhaps unrealistic to expect of anyone. I would guess that even adults don't focus uninterruptedly for six hours at work.

If we think about the school day, it is divided up into sections, often by subjects, with a break in between, each section lasting perhaps an hour, less for really young children. Within one of these subject periods there would probably be set a specific learning task after some preparation from the teacher, probably through talking. The children would then have the opportunity to work on their own at the task during which time there would be a lot of messing about. Some would finish early, some wouldn't get finished, but the amount of time they would spend actually concentrating on achieving the task would probably be quite small.

Realistically, children only focus on the work in hand for small periods – maybe no more than minutes – and the tasks they are set to do don't take that much time, and take even less time in an environment where there are not 29 other children to distract them. So when home educating, it may work better to approach your children's 'work' time from the perspective of achieving the activity rather than a set number of hours.

As children home educating can get through tasks much quicker, it often happens that they progress at a faster rate. But it also means that they have more time for other activities, such as playing as discussed before. Having extra time for play is not something you need to worry about, for if you remember, it is these alternate and self-led activities that helps children's development as much as focused learning.

> *Make sure you're not expecting too much work time from them – remember a walk in the park with an enthusiasm to look around you and learn will be worth more than two hours whingeing at home.*
>
> **Parent of six children, home educating for 15 years**

Another advantage of being relaxed about your use of time is that children can have longer to really grasp a concept that they might not have had time for in school. Many children say that the teacher had rushed ahead before they really understood a topic. When home educating, your child can have as much time as they need to understand fully. Using time in this flexible way makes best use of the opportunity to remove time restrictions on your child's day that may inhibit their learning.

During the school day there would be lots of time wasted moving between rooms, waiting for the class to settle between activities, while disruptive children are being dealt with, materials found, waiting for the teacher; time filled with other activities designed to keep children occupied but not intently learning. No child turns up at school and learns from nine till three. So there is no need to worry that you need to keep your child intently 'working' from nine till three at home. Instead, you have the opportunity to use this extraneous time much more productively. It is far more valuable for your child to be engaged on an activity of their choosing, even though it might be a computer game or playing, than it is waiting for their peers to settle or while Sir deals with a miscreant!

Another time aspect to consider is that learning can go on after school hours; it can happen anywhere, any time, anyhow. A visit to a battle re-enactment at the weekend is as valuable a history lesson as half an hour's study with a textbook. If you want to 'time' your child's learning will you be taking this kind of learning time off your 'working' week? Perhaps, instead, you could lose the distinctions between 'work' time and real life. This way learning becomes a relevant and integral part of life and sometimes children will not even feel they are 'working' at valuable learning. Learning does not have to be time restricted to be successful. There are occasions when it helps to have time objectives, obviously. But learning is more successful if it can take advantage of flexibility and relevance to the learner.

Another way in which parents can worry about the use of time is when they feel their children may not be achieving certain levels within certain time frameworks. In schools attainment targets are set as a very general and basic standard. Children, on the other hand, are very individual beings. Very few of them fit within this general framework. You may like to consider: does this matter? For example, some children read easily by the time they're seven or earlier. Some children don't read easily until they're teenagers. But by the time they're 21 no one would know, so does it matter?

Most of us, at some point in our lives, have difficulty learning particular skills. It is not that we are unintelligent. It's just the way we are. We have intelligence and aptitude for different things. We take longer over some things than others.

Home education gives children the opportunity to take longer to learn certain skills if they require it. It is better to use this opportunity to give your child more time than it is to worry that your child is not achieving something within a particular time scale. Home educating gives this flexibility, which for some children is exactly what they need.

Top Tip on the use of time:

Make 'time' work for your child, rather than make your child work to a time. This makes best use of the opportunity to be flexible to individual needs, which is one of the greatest advantages of home educating.

Motivation

How do you get children to work at their learning? This is one of the questions home educators get asked a lot. The answer is based on what we've already discussed about their love of learning and their curiosity. They do it because they want to. They understand the purpose, what education is for (this is discussed in more detail in Chapter 9). They have fun. Most of all, they do it because they have their innate desire to learn reignited, or never quelled in the first place. This is the key.

That doesn't mean to say that all the things that home educating parents ever give children to do are things they inherently want to do at that time. They don't. There are times when children need considerable persuading!

Their motivation is based on a mixture of other things too. It is based on:

- keeping the child's education directly *relevant* to them and their needs
- children understanding *why* they might need to do something
- *respect and communication* between children and parents, and trusting children with information
- *discussing* their education with the children, both immediate tasks and long-term effects
- children understanding that there are *payoffs* for achieving certain things, whether these are immediate extrinsic rewards (gold stars, extra playtime or pocket money, trip to the cinema) or long-term intrinsic rewards which older children can understand are directly for their benefit (good results, job satisfaction, high income, fulfilment, health and happiness)
- *negotiation* and *compromise* between parents and children
- keeping it as light, *stimulating* and fun as is possible, rather than over serious, heavy going and dull
- children seeing education as an integral part of, and a way of *enhancing*, their lives, rather than something tedious to be finished with as soon as possible
- making children feel that they have some *control* over their education
- bringing *contrast and variation* to their activities. Using some of the various ways in which children can learn described above will

help bring a contrast and balance between activities. This will help prevent their education from becoming stale and samey. We are all more motivated when we have variety and balance: for example, indoor/outdoor activities, academic/practical, sedentary/physical, focused/relaxed.

Children feeling that they really can have some say in their education, rather than always being at the mercy of what others say, probably has the greatest effect on their motivation and personal development.

A PERSONAL STORY

I believe that the greatest advancement in our children's home education and their maturity came when they finally understood something different about education to that which they had first believed when they were in school. They discovered that education, instead of being something that was 'done to' them by others often in unpleasant ways, was something enjoyable that they could be in charge of and which directly benefited them and their future in ways they could really see.

Giving children greater control over their own education is discussed next. It is all part of the *relationship* home educators develop with their children to use to keep them motivated. And that relationship is based on respect. *All* children have a right to respect. When shown respect themselves, children are more likely to have respect for others. They are also more likely to have *self*-respect. Self-respect is essential for self-motivation. Self-motivation is what will keep children learning. And it is an invaluable skill to have for life.

I home educate because my son was becoming alienated from learning. Now he can't get enough – he wants to know everything. The learning approaches I take are – English language and maths are like lessons. I really want him to be at ease with grammar, fractions etc... All other subjects are adventures whether it is science, history or geography. We use CD Roms, do experiments, go on field trips, watch DVDs.

Parent of one child, home educating for two and a half years

> ## Top Tip on motivation:
>
> Listening to your child's ideas about their education, and answering respectfully, makes them feel they are valued. Even if you don't go on to use these ideas, once they've been discussed children are much better able to compromise if they feel valued, even young children.

Children having charge of their own learning

Motivation comes from having the desire to do something. We have the desire to do something when we see a *purpose* for an activity. We feel very purposeless and unmotivated to do something if the only reason we have to do it is because we've been told to do so by someone else.

This is the same with home educating children. Constantly telling a child to do something they just don't want to do creates conflict. Involving them in the decision-making about what to do and why makes them feel more in control of it, and if they are in charge it gives them purpose. Consequently they feel more motivated.

Giving children charge of their own education is an idea most of us would be surprised by. How can we give them charge? What do they know about it? Surprisingly, children can take charge of their education and even small children can be made to feel like they have some control over it.

Obviously it is not something that can happen overnight, especially if children have had no practice. As we discussed with homework, most children have been so spoon-fed their education they would have no idea how to go about it. Actually, we parents are in a similar situation; we have been used to schools having charge of our children's education and are having to learn how to do it if we want to home educate, hence this book! But we are learning. And it is possible. Here are some ideas as to how to make children feel more in charge of their own learning.

THROUGH DISCUSSION

Rather than keeping education to ourselves like some mysterious club that children know nothing about, we can discuss all aspects of their education with our children. Discussion is the first step. Discussion about what education is and what it's for, and most of all how it benefits them. Asking them how they see it.

KEEPING IT RELEVANT TO THEM

Keeping their learning directly relevant to their everyday lives helps children to see how it benefits them. So we can involve them in discussions about why we learn something and how you might do it. This might be as simple, with a young child, as 'It's important we know how to count so that we know how many apples to buy, so what shall we practise counting with?' You could have some materials available and let the child choose. Or with an older student, 'What subjects interest you or do you think you need to go for that career and how would it be best to tackle them?' These kinds of discussion, which demonstrate that a task is relevant to them, help to make children feel in charge.

INVOLVING THEM IN DECISION-MAKING

Later on, children can be involved in decision-making about all aspects of their education: how to arrange their day; what topics to do each day; what topics they think they should cover; how much time should be spent doing them. If children are kept informed, then they can make informed decisions. Information helps them too, when it is a case of saying 'Don't you think you've spent long enough now on the Nintendo?' If they know why they need to do something else they are more likely to choose to be guided by you rather than for there to be conflict.

COMPROMISE

If children feel as if their contribution is valuable then they are more willing to compromise when it is time to say, 'Well, I think we need to spend some time this morning concentrating on our English, so how about we go out when we've finished?' This is particularly true for younger children, but as they get older it is hoped that children will see that their education is ultimately their own responsibility.

MAKING IT THEIR OWN RESPONSIBILITY

Teenagers are tricky; medical science has proved that their brains are out of sync for a while with normality. This does not mean, though, that they will not take charge of their own education. It would be more difficult for a teenager who has just come out of school where they've been told what to do, when, how and what to wear, to behave responsibly towards their work, than a child who has been home educated for a while and grown accustomed to having charge of it. But most home educators find that once their teenagers understand why they need to do stuff and how it benefits them they do take charge of it. They might not arrange it in a way we'd like them to – I have a friend whose teenager got up at midday and worked till midnight, but they still got it done. So maybe we have to compromise too. What we do need to do is trust.

TRUST

Because of our traditional views about how children learn we tend to find it surprising that they may be able to take charge of their own education. If they understand why they need to be educated, they are surprisingly able to take charge although it may not be in our way or our timescale. It is up to us to trust it will happen. And offer lots of encouragement.

ENCOURAGEMENT

Children respond brilliantly to encouragement. They respond to it far better than other methods used to get children to work like threats, ridicule or shame, shouting or a dictatorial or bullying attitude. Bullying gets children working while they're being bullied, but they cease working once the bully is removed. Encouragement to take responsibility for themselves keeps them working whether you're around or not, because they know it is for their own gain. This responsible attitude overflows into other aspects of their life.

The processes described above take some adjusting to. They may be things you find uncomfortable working with or you may find they work for your family brilliantly. It is important to try new ways when the old are not working well. It's also important to work in ways you and your family are comfortable with. The most important criterium for choosing your approach is to make the needs of your child the priority.

Top Tip on children in charge of their own learning:

Responsibility is something that children mature into. Be encouraging, involve them at every step and be patient. It helps to talk to other home educators who have older children about how they tackled it.

Opportunities within the community for learning

Home education can be a misleading title. For some home educators home is only a small part of their story.

There are a wide range of opportunities and resources within the community which families can take advantage of to stimulate, keep interest alive and support their children's learning with practical experiences. Listed below are some of them.

- *Libraries.* Not only for books, DVDs and computer access, but also for story sessions, exhibitions, research of local resources. And sometimes they have a community room where you could establish a group meeting.

- *Parks, playgrounds and indoor play centres with climbing apparatus* for physical education and social activity.

- *Community centres.* These often have local groups which meet for art and craft, sports, or other special interests. They often have pre-school group facilities which they may be willing to hire out for young children, or rooms where you can arrange informal gatherings or group activities. Look at their notice boards.

- *Museums.* As well as the usual exhibits they can also have special exhibitions and workshops and special working days.

- *Nature reserves, woodlands, wetland centres.* As well as the obvious exploration these too may have special workshops or a specialist worker at the site who can lead group activities.

- *Recycling centres.* Some of these have a scheme where a group can have membership for a small fee which then entitles them to free resources and materials. There are some surprising finds to be made!

- *Galleries.* As well as their usual exhibitions they too have special shows and sometimes professional art workers willing to lead a group activity.

- *Churches and other historic buildings.* These give opportunities for first-hand history experiences, looking at local materials and most have a local history or historic figure around which exhibitions are built.

- *Stately homes, castles and ruins.* Also period cottages and farmhouses. All offer opportunities for learning about history, social culture and geography as well as the more obvious activities. Sometimes they have special working days too.

- *Sites of specific interest.* Things like quarries, brickworks, small local reserves, Bronze Age sites, etc. all offer opportunities for learning both from a simple visit and on specialist activity days.

- *Wildlife parks or similar places of natural interest like animal sanctuaries.* Children love to visit places that have animals. These places offer lots of things to see and learning opportunities.

- *Plant centres.* Walking around a plant centre gives a great opportunity to discuss different species and plant families. Many of them have play areas attached or other centres of particular interest like pets or birds of prey or ponds, etc.

- *Bridges or other major constructions like railways, tunnels, viaducts, etc.* are all worth a visit to reinforce learning about construction, materials, forces, etc. and changes in social and industrial history.

- *Riverbanks, estuaries, streams and ponds.* These give the opportunity for learning about life in the water and the surrounding environment, as does any field trip to any natural place, beach included.

- *Theatres.* Some theatres run children's classes and workshops as well as having productions linked to the school curriculum.

- *Colleges.* Local colleges often have family workshops or professionals who would be willing to give a workshop.

- Many areas offer *swimming pools, climbing walls, ice rinks, skate parks, training grounds, rowing lakes, riding schools,* all useful for physical activity and some will offer a group reduced school rates.

- *Tourist information centres.* These provide a wealth of information about local opportunities and places to visit as well as special events like literary festivals, battle re-enactments and craft fairs.

- *Ordnance Survey maps* indicate local areas of interest plus local footpaths and bridleways and disused railway lines, useful for exploration, orienteering and outdoor activities.

Most outdoor sites have a particular geographic or natural interest or opportunities for learning. Somewhere as simple as the park can offer opportunities to study plants, trees, insects, soil, food chains, woods, birds, wildlife, conservation, ecology, habitats, environmental control and diversity. Not to mention opportunities for creative writing and artwork, making charts and tables about the things you see, collections and counting. Think how you might use railways, airports, estuaries, towns, buildings, even cemeteries, for these all offer opportunities for learning. As do other professionals you might know like potters, artists, craftsmen, musicians, nurses, specialist teachers or conservationists.

Out-and-about education would perhaps be a better title than home education. Most home educators utilise as many opportunities within their community as they can. It helps to keep the children stimulated. It gets them out of the house. It helps keep their interest in the world around them alive.

Top Tip on opportunities within the community for learning:

Keep your eyes open in your community not only for the obvious resources described above, but also for the less obvious: like perhaps the old lady who lives next door and who would love to chat to children about her experiences in the war, or someone you know who might have a special skill like a drummer or a builder.

Summary of the main points

- Children can learn in a multitude of different ways beyond our first assumptions about how they learn.

- In order to learn children need these basic things: stimuli; a comfortable learning environment; motivation; encouragement and support; confidence.

- As well as through academic study and through teaching, children can also learn on their own through: first-hand experience; trial and error; investigation; exploration; experimentation; practical practice.

- One of the best opportunities to give children first-hand experiences is through play and discussion.

- Parents who are home educating tend to view their role as more to encourage and support their children's learning, rather than to teach them.

- Giving children opportunities to practise skills is as important as giving them knowledge.

- There are many approaches home educators take to their children's learning. Keeping flexible and in tune with their children's needs is the most essential element of any approach.

- Giving children respect, keeping them informed, valuing their opinions, and keeping their love of learning alive are all ways in which home educators help to motivate their children.

- Children are more motivated to learn for themselves rather than through being taught. With the right encouragement they are well able to take responsibility for their education as they mature.

- Home educators use a wide range of opportunities within their community to support their children's learning.

Final Tip for this chapter:

Having read this section you might feel that there is a lot to take in. You don't have to know it all or do it all. You don't need to be doing all the time. What you do need to do is be patient. Dip in and try out, pare down and discard what doesn't work, or try it again at another time. Your methods and styles will evolve as you go along.

Suggested websites

Freedom for Children to Grow: www.freedomforchildrentogrow.org

National Home Education Network: www.nhen.org

Beacon-Light Education: www.beaconlightededucation.com (go through the site map to 'Home-Education')

The Link Homeschool Magazine: www.homeschoolnewslink.com (explore the articles in various issues)

Chapter 4

How Do Home Educated Children Find Friends and Become Socialised?

This chapter is about children making friends and becoming socialised. It will probably help us to understand how these things happen if we look at the issues of friendship and socialisation separately. We will look at what we know about friendships and social interaction in schools, our traditional assumptions about them, and how home educators make friends and develop their social skills.

The chapter deals with the following issues:

How children make friends pre-school

How schools do not have exclusivity on friendships

How schools can sometimes harm relationships

The importance of occasional solitude

What social skills do we want our children to have?

How children acquire social skills

How do home educated children find friends?

The home education community

Opportunities for friendships within the local community

How children make friends pre-school

Making friends and mixing successfully with others is something parents worry about a lot. Especially early on in their children's lives. We perhaps worry unduly; if we think about toddlers and children it is very rare that they remain isolated. Wherever you take them, park, playground, social get-togethers with other parents, they tend to gravitate towards one another. We just need to provide them with the opportunity to do so and set them a good example.

As parents we're generally advised to get our young children to nursery, toddler and pre-school groups to find them friends and get them mixing with others. This has led parents to believe that this is the *only* way children find friends and become socially adept.

These groups certainly are a good place to find playmates, meet others, and begin to build a friendship group. But it is important to realise that they are not the only place to do so. Children also find friends through family gatherings, through parents' friends and neighbours, through other activities like Tumble Tots, music groups, swimming groups, at the library story sessions. In other words, all the normal interaction anyone would have in any community. The more children and parents are out and about in the community the wider their friendship network becomes. It is not the case that children only have friends if they belong to a nursery or school type institution.

Parents are also sometimes led to believe that their children at this stage should be successfully mixing, chatting, sharing and getting along with others. But this is rather an unrealistic expectation.

There is no doubt that children need to integrate with others. We all do. It enhances our lives. It might help us though to review our idea of whether integrating small children with others of a similar age actually 'socialises' them. For copying the behaviour of other children who are too immature to be sociable themselves is not likely to teach our child the refined skills we want them to have. Nor do children of this age have the skills needed to form good relationships with others.

So in reality, it is quite rare that children form and keep strong specific friendships pre-school. All children are different; some children are just not mixers, some children don't enjoy larger groups, some children are sensitive to noise and some children are very happy in their own company. High expectations about friendships and socialisation skills in young children at this stage can cause unnecessary worry.

All that children need are *comfortable* social experiences so that they become increasingly comfortable in social situations, whether they have friendships at this stage or not. And home educators find that these experiences are not exclusive to schools, pre-schools and nurseries. They can just as easily be formed outside those institutions.

How schools do not have exclusivity on friendships

> We meet regularly with a home educating group and individual families on a regular basis and the children have made some good friendships, so they are not cut off and isolated as is often suggested. As they are frequently in contact with adults on a social level they are all able to speak confidently, coherently and appropriately to people of all ages, which is often commented upon when we are out and about.
>
> Parent of three children, home educating for seven years

Our traditional assumption that friendships are dependent on children going to school has evolved because mostly we don't look beyond it.

Children make friends in school because they happen to be in school. Home educators find that they can also make friends just as easily when they happen to be in other places, like youth centres for example. School has simply become a convenient gathering of children where friendships inevitably form. But whilst children are in school they do not have the opportunity for other social interaction. Home educated children can develop a social circle outside school simply by being given the opportunity to do so.

> We joined local Education Otherwise groups for activities and socialising, but my son also had a selection of other activities and clubs over the years, like Cubs/Scouts, swimming, snooker, weight training, badminton, youth club, so he gathered a wide range of interests and friends outside the home educating circle.
>
> Parent, home educating for ten years

If we think about it, if schools had exclusivity on friendships it would be a bit tough on the rest of us who've finished with school. It would assume that no one made friends after they left, which we know is not true. So how do the rest of us make friends as adults? Are the only friends we have friends that we found at school?

Most adults have a wide social group which has nothing to do with being at school. We make friends through the normal interaction we have in our everyday lives, our work, our family and social activities, our interests. The Internet has broadened that even further via email, chat rooms and web groups.

So realistically we all, children included, can make friends as much outside of school as within it, given the opportunity to do so. Not going to school does not automatically mean that children will be without friends. In fact, it sometimes happens that the interaction in school can be more harmful than life enhancing because the school climate is such that it is not always conducive to fostering loyal and supportive relationships.

The next section discusses how this can happen.

How schools can sometimes harm relationships

Many people believe that school is an example of the norm of social interaction, but we might want to reconsider whether it is.

For example there is rarely anywhere else outside of school where:

- you come across enforced age-restrictive grouping
- you might be laughed at or considered abnormal if you want to interact with other people who are not of the same age
- gangs and cliques are prevalent and bullying is common
- you are forced to be with the same group for a long period of time irrespective of choice.

Even in work, where we have to tolerate colleagues we may find challenging, we still ultimately have a *choice* to change our job if it becomes unbearable. Children in school have no access to these choices. Choice affects relationships, as do many other factors found in a school environment. These are described below.

CLIMATE AND ENVIRONMENT

Children in school are forced into unnatural social groupings where they have no choice about changing if they are harassed, bullied, made to feel bad about themselves or excluded and isolated. Even worse, they have to endure this same group usually for their entire school life. These enforced groupings, often based on age, can be fiercely competitive and threatening. This is seldom a comfortable climate where friendships can be formed out of a positive attraction or mutual interest. The enforced grouping is not a good example of life outside school. Even the climate of adult and child relationships can become one of great tension as teachers are forced into strategies of child control rather than relationship building. This is not the best environment for maturing good relationships.

TOO LITTLE QUALITY ADULT INTERACTION

To learn about and forge good quality relationships and friendships children need good quality relationships around them to emulate. Most importantly from *adults*. They need lots of examples. Often, because of the way in which schools are set up with one or two adults in charge of 30 or more, sometimes resentful or disruptive, children, the behaviour that the adults have to resort to is not a good example of respectful or quality interaction. Caring relationships are often sacrificed to the need for mass control.

UNHEALTHY COMPETITIVE CLIMATE

We always come across competition in our lives and inevitably have to compete in order to get anywhere. Some adults feel that the nature of competition in schools is a good example of the nature of competition in life ahead and it is a good learning opportunity when their children are exposed to it. What is often overlooked is the matter of *choice*. Most adults, in their lives outside school, choose whom to compete with, when and in what circumstances. They also have the option to withdraw if they feel like it. This choice is not afforded to children in school and it is the lack of that choice that can sometimes make relationships in school become desperate. Education need not be a competitive race; it is a personal quest. When education is set up as a race to beat others, by both schools and parents, it loses its intrinsic value to the learner. It puts strain upon any relationships that the learner might have in school and it can easily destroy self-esteem. Poor self-esteem leads to poor relationships and ultimately poor achievement.

DESPERATION OF BELONGING TO A GROUP

We all have the need to belong to a group. We choose to belong to groups out of mutual interests or attraction. Children in schools can feel the need to be in a group purely out of desperation and fear of being on the outside, rather than for any positive reasons that would enhance their relationships. Obviously fear and desperation are not the best criteria for forging good relationships within a group. Groupings in school are often quite narrow, and it can become very hard for those children whose individualism makes it difficult for them to fit. Out of school children have wider opportunities for finding groups that suit them, rather than trying to make themselves fit a group.

FEAR AND SHAME OF FAILURE

In some schools there is a definite stigma attached to not achieving. And some teachers can make children feel bad if they don't understand a topic quickly. In order to reach their potential children need to feel good at all times about learning. They need to feel that whatever they achieve – or don't achieve – there is no need to feel shame or fear. They need to have confidence not only in their learning but also in the *people* who are facilitating it. Confidence is a key element to creating good relationships. In turn, good relationships are a key element to learning. Fear, shame, anxiety about failure, humiliation or degradation damages both relationships and achievement.

MOST IMPORTANT OF ALL: RESPECT

It is often said that children do not respect adults any more. If you look around at some of the adult behaviour it is not difficult to see why. Respect needs to be earned. It is also a *two-way* thing. Children who are not respected themselves, most particularly by the people who have charge of them and their education and who they are supposed to be able to trust, are not going to learn the good things about respect. *Mutual respect is paramount to good relationships.* Disrespectful behaviour destroys relationships and overflows into many other aspects of life. Children need to understand respect by having it demonstrated to them. Sadly, some desperate adults in schools resort to disrespectful behaviour. Worse still, they cover up that disrespect by abusing their powerful positions. Children know more than adults like to think about who deserves respect or not. Because of the school environment where there are enforced situations, a huge institutional agenda instead of intimate personal relationships, unnatural groupings, lots of children with too few adults, there is not always enough opportunity to make the relationships within schools respectful ones.

These are some of the factors that explain why some of the social interaction within schools is at times undesirable or of such poor quality it is damaging to the learner. When home educating many of these factors can be removed.

> *Our daughter still had moments of wanting to go to school again, especially around the time when she would have moved on to secondary school. But before long, one particular friend told her of the bullying and tormenting that she was suffering. She was having to change her behaviour and start swearing in order to be like the others. One of the most common arguments that we hear against home education is that if children don't go to school they miss out on the social aspects. What social aspects are those, we ask! If you're thinking about home education but worry about the social bit, don't worry. Your children don't need it! There will be plenty of opportunities, either in further education or at work, to socialise without the unhappiness that (sadly) is often associated with school these days.*
>
> Parents of two children, home educating for nine years

It helps anyone considering home education to be aware that, in the end, being surrounded by large numbers of children does not necessarily guarantee that a child will have large numbers of friends or good quality relationships. And perhaps large numbers of friends is not as desirable as a small trustworthy group, or even just one. One quality relationship can be more meaningful than a mass of enforced acquaintances. These are important points to keep in mind.

What is also important and equally underestimated is that, like adults, as well as social interaction children need to have moments of solitude sometimes denied them during a school life. The next section explains why.

The importance of occasional solitude

Most of us have a painful mental image of our child standing in the school playground alone whilst others have groups of friends all around them. It's probably one of our biggest fears. Traditionally, as soon as a teacher or supervisor saw this they'd be trying to integrate the child into a group somewhere.

It is of course important that children integrate. It's equally important that children are allowed to be solitary at times if they so desire it without feeling that there is something wrong with being on their own.

Solitude is something that many people are wary of. It conjures up an impression of a Billy-no-mates or a wallflower. It reinforces the generalisation that being with a group is always desirable and always healthy, another generalisation which fails to incorporate the idea that everyone is an individual and not everyone fits in with a general view.

Some children are very gregarious. They enjoy mixing with others, find it easy, get along with others easily and like lots of company all of the time. They have no problem with large groups, shyness or crowded places.

Other children are not. They do not enjoy large groups, crowded places or the press of people and hubbub that goes with them. Some adults are the same and we allow them their right to be as they are. It is important to remember to afford the same right to children and not to believe there is something wrong with them, or make the child feel that there is something wrong with preferring their own company.

Most children feel frightened and daunted by the general mayhem of the school playground. Probably most adults do too, although they don't admit to it! School can be a frightening and daunting place and it's natural to take some time getting used to it. It is also just as natural if a child *doesn't want* to get used to it or prefers smaller, more intimate groups, or long periods of time in their own company.

✻

Different children have different preferences.

✻

Sometimes their preference for solitude is disregarded within the school environment or seen as a fault.

It is important that we give our children the opportunity to mix. Equally children should be afforded the right *not* to mix at times and that we appreciate that lone time is valuable. We should never make children feel inadequate for being as they are out of *our own adult* desperation that they should belong.

Many creative, philosophic or scientific achievements have probably depended upon adults having lone time. Solitude is an important opportunity for children to review, to think, to daydream. It is now understood that children need time for daydreaming, time when they are not in school, hanging out with others or stuck in front of a computer. They need solitary time to enhance their imaginative skills, for the development of thinking and reasoning, to make sense of the things they have learned and their experiences. Children who are at school rarely have the opportunity to do this, or to make the choice not to mix at times without being ridiculed.

Home education gives children the opportunity to have the interaction (or not) which suits their particular needs. No one would want their child to become totally introverted or unable to mix at all. But occasional solitude does not mean that this will happen and need not be a cause for worry. Occasional solitude is as important for development as social interaction is.

What social skills do we want our children to have?

To understand how to develop social skills in our children we need to identify what those skills are. What do we want our children to be able to do?

We'd probably answer that question by saying that we want our children to be comfortable with others, to have nice manners and behave nicely in public, thus making them well liked! But we need to be more specific. What is behaving nicely and having nice manners all about?

Behaving 'nicely' is really about children's responses to a social situation. For example, in a relaxed social setting it is okay to lark about and play. On a more formal occasion, maybe a visit to someone whom you don't know very well, who has a neat and tidy house, you'd like the children to behave. And by behave you probably mean that you'd like them to be able to speak to people comfortably, show consideration for their home and the people in it until you learn their rules.

Behaving nicely and good manners boils down to respect and consideration for others. That's all it is. It's about understanding that auntie doesn't like it when you swear or put your feet on her settee, so out of respect and consideration for her you refrain from doing this until you're with your mates. It's about understanding that it makes John feel sad when you call him names, so out of consideration for him you don't do it. It's about understanding that when someone speaks to you it's considerate to answer, or to wait until someone else has finished talking until you speak. Little things like that.

This is what we need to be explaining to our children. We need to be explaining that behaving nicely is not about boring adults being old fashioned. It's about showing consideration and respect for others. Showing consideration and respect for others makes you a nice person, makes you popular, makes you friends.

That's what children need to understand about being sociable. We want our children to be considerate and to make judgements about what's appropriate in a variety of social settings and to respond in a considerate way. They need confidence to do this. They need self-esteem.

So we're talking about:

- making the right responses
- showing consideration and behaving appropriately
- having confidence
- being articulate.

How do we get our children to that point?

How children acquire social skills

So how do we give our children confidence in social settings, get them to use consideration? How do they become articulate and understand what appropriate behaviour is? Simple:

✳

By a good example – a good *adult* example.

✳

Most of us have been led to believe that children become socialised by being in school with other children.

But being with other children only teaches children how to be with other children. And most other children do not possess the refined skills we want our children to develop. Being with other children in school does not necessarily teach children those social skills we want them to develop in order to function socially in the world *outside* school.

This is why it is rather ironic that would-be home educators worry that their children's social development will be impaired if their child does not go to school. Far from being impaired it is likely to be enhanced, simply because most home educated children mix with a greater proportion of adults. Most adults demonstrate respect, care and attention and have the time to guide children in developing their social skills. And those adults also have greater opportunity to build children's confidence and self-esteem by giving them respect and making them feel *they matter*.

Children in schools where there are huge numbers of children to too few adults rarely have that kind of interaction. Teachers rarely have that kind of time. Children's social skills in school sometimes become pared down to the simple strategy of surviving among a mass of unsociable beings generally only intent on their own advancement, whatever the cost to others. Confidence can be fragile.

If children were constantly in the company of other respectful, caring and considerate adults and children, in a variety of social experiences, they would mostly become respectful, caring and considerate themselves. Mostly it is the case that children learn social behaviour by having it demonstrated to them. And they learn anti-social behaviour by having it demonstrated to them – they rarely think it up for themselves or make individual choices when at the mercy of pressure from a group. If we want our children to behave like responsible, respectful adults then they need the company of responsible, respectful adults from which to learn it. It is as simple as that. They learn by our example.

It has been observed that home educated children seem to have greater social aptitude than their school peers. This is simply to do with the fact that they have much more social interaction with far more adults and less time spent with large numbers of unsupervised children who have limited social skills.

Home education gives parents much better control over providing good quality, respectful, considerate social experiences for their children. It gives them opportunities to discuss the way they see people behaving, to take responsibility for making choices about the way they behave.

People often comment on the children's sociability and confidence in talking to others. One lady, at a wood craft course we have been attending, said that she had been about to ask me about the familiar socialisation aspect of home education, but changed her mind when she realised it clearly wasn't an issue!

If I'm totally honest, it is their social life that wears me out the most! Both children are real 'people people', and so like to 'get out there' at any opportunity. We have been very fortunate that we moved to an area where there was such an active home education group, when we started down the home education route. The children have made some really close friends through the group, and one of them commented recently that he feels so much part of things there, something which he didn't ever feel at his last school.

Parent of two children, home educating for three years

How do home educated children find friends?

Home educated children find friends in the same way as you or I find friends. You and I still have friends even though we do not go to school. We find friends through our normal daily interaction: work, interests, sport, social activities, local groups, Internet contacts.

Home educated children find friends in similar ways. Some have friends from early interaction, pre-school groups, nursery or school if they attended them; from the neighbours, parents' acquaintances, street, village. Some have friends from clubs, groups, classes, workshops or parties they've attended. Some have friends through particular interests like riding or playing football, for example, dance or playing pool.

The more the children are involved in activities outside the home the wider their social circle becomes. Children who are not in school are not automatically isolated. This is an adult assumption that is the result of generalised thinking. Few, if any, families home educate in isolation. Sometimes in rural communities that are less populated it is more difficult to find groups of children to mix with, but this is as much to do with remote areas as to whether the children are home educated or not.

Home educators also find friends among other home educating families, by attending home educating gatherings and at local home educating groups. Being members of home educating organisations enables families to develop a network of other home educators both locally and further afield through pen friends and Internet groups. The home educating community is growing all the time. The next section looks at it in more detail.

> ...we meet up regularly in term time and do all sorts but in the holidays we still meet for a chat and the kids to play; quite often someone with a garden has a garden day, we did that yesterday and we still meet up in a park for picnic and play, we organise a mums' night out...and the babysitting is shared out among the partners and husbands and parents.
>
> Parent of two children, home educating for three and a half years

The home education community

The numbers of home educators are increasing rapidly as parents become more and more dissatisfied with their local schools. It seems inevitable that this will continue, so the numbers of other home educators with whom to mix is bound to expand. Thus the home educating community grows and gives a greater range of contacts and social opportunities for home educators.

There are several organisations to support home educators, the biggest being Education Otherwise, and they offer a range of opportunities. The most valuable of these is the network of contacts, usually in the form of a list of other home educators exclusive only to members. Members keep in contact mostly through web networks and meetings. Through these networks home educating groups develop.

Groups vary depending on families' needs, who they are run by and how they are run, but most provide opportunities to meet either for social interaction or for a particular activity, outing or field trip. The groups use parents' expertise or other professionals to provide a range of educational activities, organise group trips to museums, field trips, etc. or for workshops at other venues. They may organise a party, barbecue or other celebration similar to those which children may have in schools. Or simply meet for an informal chat and mutual support.

The groups mostly have a high proportion of adults to children, as most parents take full responsibility for their children and stay with them, getting involved with helping to run the group. They provide opportunities not only to learn, but also to interact with others, find friends and practise social skills. Some home educating parents set up the opportunity to take turns for responsibility for children to give each other breaks.

The common aim of the members of these local groups is to provide support to one another. So they are mostly welcoming and supportive to any home educators wishing to join.

> I've been actively involved with our local home educators' group for over eight years. When we started up there were less than half a dozen families and we met once a fortnight at a local community centre... The group stayed small for the first year or so, but we gathered more members until now there are over 50 families involved, meeting twice weekly. We had over 100 participants at one of our most recent events! The group is run organically with no structured hierarchy and all home educators are welcome to join. Consequently we have a vibrant community including people of various religions and none; vegans, vegetarians and meat-eaters; people who educate in a structured way and people who educate autonomously. We all respect each others' right to be different and

expect our children to do so – this may be why we have very little in the way of bullying.

The activities are normally provided by parents and are very varied. For example we've had a Japanese day which included silk dyeing and sushi making; we've studied rocks and fossils including going on a rock trial around our local city centre and we've had a session looking at the design and construction of cars. Occasionally we will have sessions led by outside experts, which have included African drumming and a day at the museum doing experiments with light and finding out about Galileo. Trips further afield have included the space museum at Leicester, the Imperial War museum at Duxford and Stansted Mountfitchet castle. We also go for countryside walks, and have a variety of physical activities including swimming, ice-skating and ten-pin bowling.

The group is a great support to all those who home educate in the local area. It provides a chance for parents to chat about any problems they might be having – there's nearly always someone in the group who has been through it all before – or share good ideas and sources of information. The children love to spend time with their friends, and value relationships with other children whose experience is similar to their own.

Parent of three children, home educating for ten years

As with attending any new group it can sometimes feel a bit daunting trying to integrate when you are starting out. Your ability to overcome this, and go along anyway, will be a great example to your child.

Mostly, when people get over their awkwardness and shyness, they are friendly, warm and supportive. Taking the plunge and initiating conversation, perhaps with a question about how long someone has been home educating, or something about their child, or where people travel from, etc., is the way to break the ice.

Obviously home educators all meet for the same reason: support. But even adults find it is difficult to break the ice if they are not practised at it. If everyone makes an effort to be inclusive of everyone else then difficulties are soon overcome. Interacting into these groups is a great way to demonstrate to children how to interact and initiate new friendships. Children can hardly be expected to have good social skills if the adults around them shy away from practising them. Most home educators find that any awkwardness is soon overcome.

Here are a few tips:

Many people are more friendly than they seem, they just assume everyone else just wants to keep themselves to themselves. You really have to take time to get to know them.

At one group I go to, many parents do not talk but take the opportunity to catch up on their own things. I thought at first that it was cliquey, but then I realised that it was a very good chance to catch up on my own letters, books, thinking and reading.

If you don't like the style of home education that allows the children to behave in a way you're not comfortable with, then you want to meet parents who operate in a more disciplined structured way.

I used to take my son to a formal taught class, and the problem was I was too shy to make friends with the parents who collected their children – but eventually met some elsewhere and wished I could have plucked up the courage back then to suggest a cup of tea somewhere.

People like me, who have spent many years hard at work and not socialising much, have pretty poor skills in this area. An obvious suggestion is just to ask if someone would like to go to a café.

Parent of one child, home educating for four years

Opportunities for friendships within the local community

Most home educators find many opportunities for interaction with other children within their local community. The local library is an invaluable source of information about local groups, clubs and activities that are available for children. Libraries usually have a website on their local council government website too, so those are worth investigating.

Here are some other avenues to explore:

- local classes and groups like football, dance, drama, music, art groups, riding, skating, fitness, etc.

- Cubs, Scouts, Brownies, Guides and associated activities and groups

- youth clubs

- community centres

- sports centres

- swimming pools and leisure complexes

- local paper
- notice boards. Most of the above have notice boards full of activities and group gatherings. They can also be found in doctor's surgeries, local shops, parish notice boards or other public places like bowling centres, play centres, cinemas, ice-rinks, etc.
- local tourist information centres sometimes have useful information
- galleries, theatres, arts centres and museums also have community opportunities as well as learning opportunities
- further education colleges and schools running evening classes and groups of special interest.

Some of these you'll find on websites that serve your community. For example, your local council is a good place to start, or just type your nearest town or area into Google and see what comes up. Alternatively type in a group you might be interested in, youth group or pottery classes, for example, and see what you can find.

At the end of this chapter are some to start you off.

Summary of the main points

- Children meet others through their parents' interaction within the community as well as through any groups they might belong to.
- Contrary to common assumptions, pre-schools, nurseries and schools are not the only places where children are able to make friends.
- Sometimes the climate in schools is such that it can be harmful to relationships. Home educating releases children from this pressure.
- Having time on their own is as important to children's development as being in constant company.
- Children develop good social skills by being in the company of adults and children who have good social skills themselves.
- Home educated children find friends from integrating within their local community and from groups of other home educators.

- Home educating provides the opportunity for parents to give their children good quality interaction with others.

- There is an ever-growing network of home educators where they can do this.

Suggested websites

www.[put your county here].gov.uk

All 4 Kids UK Directory: www.all4kidsuk.com

www.local.co.uk

www.upmystreet.com (use the 'find my nearest' facility)

www.ask.com

Chapter 5

What about Curriculum, Subjects and Timetables?

In this chapter we will look at:

What curriculum actually is and what it's for

How home educating parents use it – or not

How curriculum, subject division and timetables are merely tools for learning and how to use them as such

Considerations for making your own timetables

Basic subjects and how to approach them

Choosing extra subjects

Subjects that develop valuable life skills

How to use curriculum and timetables to your advantage

What curriculum actually is and what it's for

In schools curriculum seems very large and very complicated. It needn't be; it's quite simple really. Curriculum is simply the content or a course of study. Or even more simply: a set plan of activities usually to guide you towards an outcome.

The National Curriculum is set by the government to be implemented in all schools to all children at the same time in their school life. It is the plan of activities that the education department feel that children in schools should undertake in order for them to become educated. It has standardised the content of what children learn, irrespective of differences, right across the country, whereas before it was implemented this could vary from school to school even though all schools had the same aim: to enable children to gain academic qualifications. The National Curriculum was established to make sure that this variation didn't happen and that all children would receive the *same* knowledge at the *same* time. And it gave teachers set objectives to achieve with all children at specific stages in their school life.

Basically, the National Curriculum dictates the subjects that children should be taught, the related knowledge and skills and understanding in each subject, and provides attainment targets and tests to measure that this is happening within a specified time framework. This is how the National Curriculum works in schools. It was designed for school use to standardise the education all children would receive.

Some parents find the National Curriculum a valuable resource to help them home educate. Some do not and prefer to devise their own curriculum in tune with their child's development. Some use other curricula linked to other educational styles, like Montessori, for example. Some prefer not to have a pre-determined curriculum of any sort at all and allow their child to learn more spontaneously through their day-to-day activities. The next section discusses these variations.

Meanwhile if you want to learn more about the National Curriculum in detail look at the government websites at the end of the chapter.

How home educating parents use it - or not

Having a curriculum as a foundation upon which to base a child's learning can be really useful. Especially if you have no idea yourself about what your child should learn, or what you want your child to learn, when, why and how. Having the National Curriculum which sets out a course of activities that all children in school will be following at specific stages in their education can give parents building blocks on which to base their child's education at home.

Commercial workbooks, which are available in bookshops, set out exercises designed around the National Curriculum for children to pursue to develop their knowledge and skills. These build in difficulty taking children through graded steps. Some home educators find these useful and prefer to stick to this style of curriculum, working through them and therefore the National Curriculum as children would in school.

However, it is not compulsory for any parents home educating to follow the National Curriculum. Some home educators prefer to follow a curriculum they have devised themselves. They plan their activities and the content of their child's learning by starting with the child's own interests and expanding from there, looking for opportunities to practise basic skills in direct relation to this interest. For example, a child interested in football could practise all their basic skills for maths, English and science by doing a project based around it. All the research, writing, science, maths, historical factors, geography, etc. could be incorporated into it. This way the children develop skills through their intrinsic interests rather than through external pressure to cover a prescribed curriculum. This method can help maintain motivation.

The decisions parents make about the way in which they use curricula or not is usually a result of their approach to home education. Parents using a more structured approach tend to prefer a curriculum-based style of learning. Parents using a more child-orientated approach tend to be more flexible in their use of curricula, adapting their use of it, if used at all, to their specific requirements. This is quite a generalisation, however, and there are many variations within that.

We started following the National Curriculum and did so for a year. The biggest thing I found out after deregistering her from school was that our daughter was about two years behind in English and maths so we couldn't follow all of the curriculum. I must own every dyslexic programme known to man! But I discovered she has a great aptitude for science and history. She excels at anything to do with arts and crafts...

...I joined many e-groups and found them a valuable source of support and information. Most seem to follow an autonomous approach, which really would not suit either myself or my daughter. Recently I was told about a structured home educating group and I found a vast variety of alternative structured curricula to the National Curriculum.

So we have recently left the National Curriculum behind and are moving on to using a Steiner Waldorf approach. This is working well at the moment and I adapt the curriculum to suit us.

Parent of one child, home educating for over
a year, and one younger child in school

Some home educating families do not use a pre-determined curriculum at all and feel that following a curriculum that has been devised without any relation to the specific learning needs of their individual children is far too general to be useful to them. They find it too prescriptive to be relevant to their individual child's education, especially if it does not match their child's learning preferences. Indeed, many parents feel that it works much better to use a style of learning that they've devised to suit their individual child's needs, rather than one that's been devised to suit society in general.

This can often be the case for children who learn best in specifically different ways, like those with dyslexia, for example, who find the traditional style of study based heavily upon the printed word doesn't work for them. Much of the way in which the National Curriculum is designed requires dependency upon printed material and for some children this is just not the best approach to their learning. Some parents find that their children learn much more successfully when they create learning experiences individually to suit them, instead of adhering to a curriculum.

When you are considering curriculum in relation to your own home education it is perhaps worth noting that any curriculum, like the National Curriculum, which has an agenda outside a particular child, in this case to standardise the educational content across the breadth of every school in the country, cannot possibly have the intrinsic needs of the individual child at its heart. It has a generalised view of children at its heart, but as we've discussed already, children cannot always fit into a generalised view. And in some cases it is damaging to their development and education to make them do so.

Most home educators find the National Curriculum a useful point of reference. Some take it further and stick to it religiously. Some completely discard it. Most are flexible in their use of it. This makes best use of the biggest advantage of home education: to tailor your child's education to suit their needs, rather than the needs of children in general.

*

Any curriculum can be modified or devised to suit individual learning preferences.

*

Here are some flexible ways you might use the curriculum:

- Use the same content but apply different approaches to get the content across, like providing more first-hand experiences.

- Refer to the content but introduce it in relation to your child's interests when it arises.

- Use it for some subjects, like maths and English for example, but address other subjects, like art or science perhaps, in other more practical ways.

- Start out with a curriculum-based approach but introduce flexibility when your child shows individual interests.

- Alternatively, allow your child to follow their own interests then introduce curriculum when they wish to accomplish specific goals.

- Use it only for your own reference.

And here are two more important points to consider:

- Decide how important it is for you and your child to keep their education exactly parallel with children in school.

- Remember to keep your child's individual learning preferences as the priority rather than the curriculum.

It is important to remember that delivering a curriculum is *not* an education in itself – education is more than that. Curriculum is merely a *tool* to help facilitate an education and needs to be used as such. There are alternative curricula associated with other educational philosophies and schools of thought which some home educators find suit their home education methods better. It is best to look at a variety of ideas rather than just accept one. These can be found through links from some of the websites listed at the chapter endings and by talking to other home educators about what they do.

> We don't use a curriculum except for the basic stuff but even then the maths and English we do is for the real world and not for an exam. We do lots of quizzes and games; things like history, geography, biology, etc. are done on the computer through games, etc.
>
> Parent of two children, home educating for three and a half years

As a home educator a curriculum is a useful tool to help you educate your child, but try to keep the *child* as a priority over the curriculum. How best you use that tool, if you wish to use it at all, is up to you.

In the next section we'll look at this and other tools like timetables and the division of subjects.

How curriculum, subject division and timetables are merely tools for learning, and how to use them as such

There is a danger that education can become more about curriculum, timetables and subjects than about the learning and personal development of the individual.

Just as a curriculum, the National Curriculum or one of your own making, is a tool to facilitate your child's education, the practice of timetabling and of dividing subjects up separately from one another is also a tool. Both are simply devices to help facilitate an education, and need to be kept in that perspective. They are not essential to it and do not constitute an education in themselves. This point is important because it is very easy to be so busy obsessing over curriculum, timetables and covering separate subjects that real learning becomes lost.

Timetables are great for planning out when everything is going to get done. They help focus thinking. They help you aim for particular goals. They help plan out when all the activities you feel you should be doing (i.e. the ones on your curriculum) are going to get covered.

The disadvantage to timetables is that they can set boundaries to learning without you realising it. For example, it may be a day when long division is on the timetable but it is perfect weather for a field trip. Or your child has just started a creative project that needs much more time spent on it than your timetable allows. So decisions have to be made whether to stick to the curriculum timetable or to take advantage of times when your child might be best motivated to learn other things, practise other skills. Parents sometimes become worried about deviating from a structured timetable or curriculum, worried that their child's learning may suffer if they do so.

This is the time to recap on Chapter 3 about how children learn. Education that is spontaneous can be equally as valuable as that which is timetabled or on a curriculum. In fact, to take advantage of moments when your child has heightened motivation to do something, or conditions are perfect for a particular activity like a field trip or even a dash to the park, can produce some of the best learning experiences.

Most home educators find that this is where it pays to remain flexible. To remember at all times that it is you and the child who are in charge of education and not a curriculum or timetable in charge of what you do and when you do it. Remember these are merely tools that you can put down at any point and it will not be detrimental to your child if you do so. It's more likely to be of benefit. This approach to using timetables and curriculum keeps the child's needs as the priority. This also applies to the way in which subjects are usually divided up by a curriculum.

In the wider world, outside school, subjects and knowledge overlap one another. It is only for the purpose of a school style education, with a structured timetabled curriculum, that they are split. Splitting subjects up divides them into manageable chunks and attainable targets, which is useful for achieving specific outcomes like test results and exams. But in the world at large knowledge seldom exists in isolation. For instance, it's hard to fully understand the geography of a location without the history of how it evolved; there's as much science involved in mixing colour as there is creativity.

Everything relates to everything else. Subjects learned in isolation from one another can become unrelated. This is why schoolchildren sometimes feel that what they learn in school has no relevance to them. They seldom see how separate bodies of knowledge fit together or fit into their world.

The strategy of dividing subjects is another tool to facilitate a learning programme. As with curricula, or timetables, it is not necessarily an essential tool. Splitting subjects up is simply another method schools use to fit learning into a structured curriculum, to be implemented via a specific timetable, for the sake of attaining set targets with large numbers of children. It does not necessarily mean those children are learning the knowledge associated with the subject. Nor does it guarantee an education.

Some home educating families who take a structured approach to their children's education find that splitting subjects up into a timetabled curriculum is the easiest way to tackle learning at home and keep a parallel with learning in school. Subject division, use of curricula and timetables are useful ways to schedule learning when a child is working towards an exam, for example.

Other home educating families do not feel they need to keep a parallel with school, in fact consider that to do so hampers their child's education, and like to approach learning in a broader, more project-orientated way or more spontaneously from their child's interests. Both styles have been known to be successful.

Some families adapt all strategies as and if it suits them, using elements of curriculum, subject division and timetabling as tools when it helps, or making their own.

The next section looks at doing that.

Considerations for making your own timetables

Most home educators devise their own timetables to suit their family routines, the activities or curriculum content they wish to cover, skills they want their children to practise and their children's individual learning preferences.

Without considering content for the moment, there are several practical elements you might like to keep in mind when making your own timetables:

- *When your child learns best.* Are they bright in the morning or difficult to get going? This may affect how you want to plan your day.

- *How they learn best.* Do they need lots of practical activity in their timetable or do they learn well in an academic way? Or perhaps a balance of both.

- *How long are they realistically able to focus* on an activity before needing an alternative?

- *What other family routines do you need to incorporate?* Things like work, other children, household jobs, etc.

- *Do you want flexibility in your timetable* for activities to be extended if required?

- *It may be that a 'timed' table of activities is not as workable for you as a simple list of activities or subjects* you want to cover each week; the time or day not being as important as what gets done.

- Consequently the *'time' on a timetable does not necessarily have to be clock time!*

- *Timetables can be designed for yearly use,* or termly, or monthly, weekly or day to day. It's up to you.

- *Does your child have needs that respond well to a specifically structured timetable?* For example, some children like rigid structures or frameworks even if 'free time' is timed into it.

- *Does your child work best with spontaneously originated activities* as they arise and find imposed structure difficult?

- *Introduce compromise between activities* you feel your child should do and activities they want to do and discuss these elements with them. This makes them feel involved and therefore more motivated.

A PERSONAL STORY

Throughout our eight years of home educating we've devised many a timetable and discarded many a timetable. Early on we made a table of a week's activities to ensure we made time to practise all the basic skills. These also had outings and physical activities on them. From there we moved on to lists of subjects, both academic skills and children's personal interests, we felt it was important to incorporate into every week, without relation to time. These were always designed in consultation with the children. Some days these timetables were followed. Other days we had other activities and we returned to them later. We kept the use of timetables as a tool to enable us to reach an outcome, revising them to suit the current objective and demonstrated the use of them to the children as such. As our eldest daughter matured, she continued with this practice and devised her own work schedules to enable her to achieve a specific outcome (completion of a course, for example). She included both the basic skills she wanted to continue and the study of subjects she wanted to pursue for her future. She imposed a structure on herself that moved her towards her set goals. She now continues this practice in college having made the transition from learning at home to learning in an institutionalised environment completely easily. (In fact, perhaps better than some of her peers who have had timetables thrust upon them without consultation and consequently have no idea how to organise their work time or set personal goals.)

Home educating gives the opportunity to devise timetables to suit your child's and family circumstances. It also gives the opportunity to educate without timetables if that works best, or to introduce them as and when they're useful, redesigning as children develop.

When home educating, parents can be completely flexible about both the time and content of their children's learning. Content is discussed in the next sections.

I feel that learning is about the world around us, so we have some formal lessons but we also spend time watching our bugs in the bug dome and things like that...

...Timetables last until they become a chore and then a new one is formed. This does not mean there is any less English or maths; it simply means that they are done in different order or different times.

Parent of one child, home educating for two and a half years

Basic subjects and how to approach them

There are three core subjects on the National Curriculum that have become the foundation of children's learning in school. These are literacy, numeracy and science.

Most home educators feel that it is important that children have the basic skills associated with these subjects, i.e. reading, writing, understanding of maths and understanding of their world. The way in which they tackle these subjects varies with each individual approach.

Many home educators use graded workbooks. These workbooks can be very helpful for those parents who find tackling these subjects daunting or who are unsure of which skills and knowledge their children need. Most workbooks are produced in accordance with the National Curriculum and in style and approach are similar to the way in which children would be working in school.

Using workbooks ensures that all aspects of a subject on the National Curriculum are covered without parents having to worry that their children are missing out on a particular subject or topic. They are graded to match children's ages and the key stages recognised in schools. They are usually self-explanatory or come with a study book containing more in-depth information.

Since workbooks cover all aspects of the National Curriculum so completely this saves parents who wish to follow it from having to devise activities for their children's education themselves.

Unfortunately there are certain pitfalls to the sole use of workbooks that you may like to keep in mind:

- Workbooks are mostly academic and therefore sometimes lack the opportunity for practical or experiential learning.

- Workbooks depend heavily on the printed word and are therefore not always useful to all children, like those with dyslexic tendencies for example.

- Children can become easily bored with learning through them as they are not as stimulating as first-hand practical approaches.

- Sometimes, in attempts to be appealing, the workbooks contain cartoons or other distractions which pull the learner away from focus on the content.

- Workbooks are very age-orientated and generalised. This can make learners (and parents) feel that they should be performing particular skills at a particular age. This is obviously not in tune with each individual child's learning differences and personal progress.

- Solely using workbooks could not be considered a complete and rounded education.

- They sometimes lack enough opportunity to re-practise and return to a subject to reinforce learning.

- Filling a workbook can be misleading in terms of achievement – a full workbook does not necessarily mean a topic has been learned or understood.

- Workbooks lack the spontaneity of using learning opportunities derived from the children's interest and are therefore unrelated to them personally; consequently many children have no intrinsic motivation to complete them.

It is so important to remember that a completed workbook does not guarantee an education. Workbooks are mostly full of academic exercises and information. But as we discussed in the chapter on learning, some of the most valuable lessons learned come through practical, first-hand experiences, questioning, experimentation and discussion, and few children learn well in a purely academic way.

Most home educators use workbooks in some way with their children at some time. But most are flexible with their use, supporting their children's understanding and experience of a subject in other ways too.

Some flexible ways you might use workbooks are:

- Use them for parent reference.

- Add to them with other exercises.

- Reinforce the use of them with real life experiences of a subject.

- Dip into them when you feel there's a shortfall in what you've covered.

- Use the best bits; skip the bits that don't work for your child.

- Allow your children to choose, doing the bits that appeal and covering the rest in other ways.

- Use them simply as a backup to what you already provide.

Some home educating families prefer not to use workbooks at all and tackle basic skills by giving their children first-hand experiences of a subject and devising their own ways to practise it. They use the experiences of others, CD Roms and Internet learning resources and their own methods and experiences to help them find ways to do this. They find that workbooks restrict their child's experience of learning by sticking closely to the National Curriculum and therefore missing other opportunities to learn that are all around them. They prefer to cover essential skills by making them a natural part of their child's everyday life.

For example, with reading, rather than stick to a reading scheme they introduce their child to reading by reading aloud to them and gradually encouraging them to read words for themselves using a variety of reading material, books, comics, magazines, computer games, any print that's around them at any time like food packets, lists, notices, etc. With writing, rather than completing English exercises parents encourage their children to write in their own ways, maybe letters, stories, emails, MSN, and develop language and vocabulary through personal use. With maths parents feel that involving children in everyday activities in the home like budgeting, shopping, management of pocket money, cooking, planning, can give children a good grounding of all the basic skills. With science parents may give their children a wide range of practical activities and expose them to topics through discussion and personal experience as we discussed in the chapter on how children learn. Much of the understanding of scientific principles can be learnt in this way.

Thus some home educators feel that basic skills can be learned through their children's daily lives and activities. This method is a much more child-orientated approach to core subjects rather than an academic approach. It delivers an education that is more directly related to their children's needs and interests at the time and consequently has more impact. Something that a pre-determined curriculum can fail to do. Some parents continue to home educate their children in this way until the children reach a point where they want to introduce more academic learning for themselves (if at all). Some parents feel that children learn all they need *when they feel the need* to for themselves. And when children see the need for themselves, they can apply themselves to structured or academic learning methods without any difficulty. This has been proved by teenagers whose parents claimed they sat around doing seemingly very little for much of their time then decided they were going to take exams and get to university…and they did!

Some home educating families have found that as their children mature and develop they begin to better understand how applying themselves to academic study helps them achieve certain goals, like qualifications or college entry for example. At this point they are better able to find the motivation to do the things they may have earlier been resistant to. Too much academic pressure too soon is likely to harm that motivation. Some parents believe that it is not valuable, or acceptable, to coerce children into activities that they have no interest in and consider that it is more likely to damage their desire to learn, than it is to develop their education. Families have shown that it is equally possible through this approach to go on to gain entry into university or work, as some have done, as it is through a more recognised academic approach pursued over most of their childhood.

These families have indicated that it is very much a matter of *trust*. Parents can become over obsessed with their children learning particular skills, by particular ages and in a particular way – namely the way they do so in school. But home educators demonstrate that less pressurised ways of learning can be equally successful and have the same outcomes, whether that is college or university entrance, qualifications, or work.

The advantage of home educating is that parents have the opportunity to try a variety of approaches to find one that suits their child best. There is no need for any child to achieve specific skills or knowledge by specific ages. And simply because they haven't done so by the time another child has does not indicate that they never will. Some children learn things in infancy. Other children don't learn the same things until they're teenagers. By the time they're 20 no one could tell the difference.

✳

Each child's education is personal to them.

✳

Home education allows the opportunity to keep it so whatever approach parents decide to take.

When deciding how to approach basic skills it may be helpful to keep the following considerations in mind:

- Identify the important skills you want your child to have.
- Which approach to learning these skills do you feel confident with?
- Through which approach does your child learn best?
- All children learn at different rates and there is no need to achieve them within specific time frameworks.

- Basic skills can be effectively learned through everyday activities as well as through a structured timetabled approach.

- Keep in contact with other home educators and what they do.

- Continually research and review a variety of ideas.

- Keep your child's needs central to your approach rather than a generalised view of children.

- As your child develops your approach may need to change.

- It is not essential to stick to the core subjects on the National Curriculum, nor the methods of achieving them or the timescale.

It is interesting to think through quite carefully at this point what it is *you* feel your children should learn about, what they should know and be able to do, independent of curriculum. Think about which skills you want them to have and *why*, based on their individual needs both *right now* and in the future. Think about what it is you feel will set them up for a happy and successful life. For the answer to these questions is basically what educational content is all about and it will help you make decisions about subjects, curriculum, approaches and core skills. These issues combine to make your own educational philosophy. Your educational philosophy will be what governs your approach and it can be personal to you. This is raised again throughout the book.

Next we'll look at choosing other subjects.

Choosing extra subjects

As we've discussed it is not required that home educators adhere rigidly to the content of the National Curriculum. This means that parents can give some serious thought as to *what* extra subjects you might encourage your child to do, and *why*. It means that home educating families have a greater choice.

Some families do base these choices on the National Curriculum if they are using it. Children in schools would be covering languages, sciences, arts, history and geography, information and communication technology (ICT), citizenship and physical education. Some families choose to study a selection of these, especially if they are working towards GCSEs or other qualifications.

In other families subject choice is based solely on the interests of the child and not for a prescribed outcome. This is more usual where they have had a more autonomous approach throughout their home education, where the child has had choice over the activities they do and when they do them.

Decisions are also affected by how long a family has been home educating, whether a child had started GCSE courses in school, whether they are working towards qualifications or not.

Following are some things to think about when deciding which subjects to study:

FOR CHILDREN OF A YOUNG AGE

- Rather than think about 'subjects' think what interests your child *now* and what they enjoy doing.

- Can you take advantage of those interests and introduce a wide variety of experiences and skills?

- Can you choose subjects full of practical experience, which all young children need?

- What do you think are essential skills and understanding for *now* as much as for the future? This helps to keep your child's learning relevant to them.

- Is there a balance in the subjects you're tackling between the more sedentary activities (like writing) and the more physical (like learning through play)?

FOR OLDER CHILDREN

- What do they enjoy doing; are they beginning to show specific interests in any subjects?

- What are their gifts and strengths?

- Do they yet have an idea about what they might want to do later in life in terms of further education or work and are there subjects you'd like to approach with that goal in mind? (It can always change.)

- Have you got a combination of subjects that brings a balance to your child's education? E.g. sciences/arts, or perhaps subjects not always easily available in schools like a sport or psychology.

- Does your child respond best to subjects that are practical, academic, physical, vocational, or a mix?

Contrary to what you might expect, local authorities tend to prefer that children are exposed to a *broad* range of activities and do not necessarily want parents to confine themselves to the core subjects or to purely academic ones. They also like to see physical activity and involvement with others. So these too are considerations.

Choosing what to study is very much a matter of personal choice. Many home educators believe that subject content in itself is not as valuable as the skills that children need, like study skills, for example. This brings us back to the earlier discussion about skills and knowledge. Many of the subjects designed for children in schools are knowledge based and purely for the purpose of passing exams and gaining qualifications. Some families feel that concentrating on these outcomes leaves gaps in the skills their young people need for their life ahead, skills like being able to research and decide, being able to converse confidently, being able to think out solutions when there are difficulties, being able to take charge and responsibility for themselves, to think creatively and effectively. These are skills that enable young people to take part in the world successfully. And many home educators base their choice of what, why and how to study around encouraging their children to develop these skills as well as simply studying to take exams.

The next section looks at some of the ways in which they do this.

Subjects that develop valuable life skills

Increasingly, employers and universities are complaining that the young people who come to them come with handfuls of qualifications but with few skills to do anything with them. They come lacking the life skills to put what they've already achieved in their education to good use.

What do we mean by life skills? We mean skills that enable us to use what we know to lead an effective life, like the example of nutrition we looked at in Chapter 3 in which children cover the subject academically but fail to see the connection between that knowledge and keeping themselves healthy. Another example would be a person who is unable to solve a problem because it isn't a multiple-choice answer! Or someone who has a maths GCSE yet who cannot manage their budget competently. Life skills are what turn simply *having* an education into education being a *tool* you can do something with in your own life.

Studying disassociated subjects in an academic way to gain qualifications sometimes fails to develop these life skills in young people. A packaged and prescriptive schooling, in a school away from real life, has little chance of doing so if you think about it. For it is being out in real life, using a variety of knowledge and skills, not simply those on an academic curriculum, which develops children's aptitude.

Home educators find that taking children out into the world around them, observing and discussing what they see, how it relates to them, how it affects their world and how in turn they can have an effect upon their world, their responsibility to it, as an individual and as part of a society, helps develop this ability to apply what they learn in a wider situation and to understand why they should learn. It gives children opportunities to *respond* to the things they know, the things they see, and how everything relates.

✳

Responding is when the learning is taking place.

✳

Equally, the things we do in our everyday lives, the caring, cooking and homekeeping; our adult work; raising a family and caring for others; using local facilities; interacting within a community; volunteering; interests and hobbies, outings and social activities, may appear mundane and seemingly uneducational. But they are all opportunities to observe, analyse, think, decide, form opinions, solve problems, interpret actions of others, be self-aware, interact, review, converse, discuss, take responsibility, all of which are essential life skills.

Subjects and activities that children are interested in and motivated to pursue themselves are similarly valuable opportunities to enhance life skills, even if it is only the opportunity to make a decision about it. Just because the child chooses an activity does not make it any less valuable educationally. What makes it educationally valuable in terms of life skills is the *understanding* of how learning *relates* to them. And understanding is developed from all the thinking out loud, the decision-making, the discussion, the questioning, the observations a child makes as a result of *being interested and making that decision*.

This is why letting them choose is important. It helps keep their love of learning alive. It contributes to the development of life skills, creates a habit for life. For to be successful and happy, they will want to learn *all* their life – not just for now.

These skills could be developed in school. But in reality, with time and curriculum restrictions, many of the activities that develop these aspects are being squeezed out of the school day in favour of a heavier academic workload. Creativity is such an activity.

Creativity, like science, is another open-ended subject that is in danger of being presented so academically it loses its opportunities to develop useful life skills. Creativity is often limited to the art lesson, painting and drawing and academic study of artists, which narrows it even further.

Hardly a day passes in our lives when we are not required to use our creative skills. Just as hardly a day passes when we do not need to use our understanding of science, even though we may not realise it.

We use our creative skills to do something as simple as making our meals, balancing our budget, or doing something more complicated like creating happy and balanced lives. All require us to think, weigh out possibilities, make decisions, solve problems. Basically we have to create our way through our lives making our homes, doing our jobs, raising our children, using our spare time. Creative thinkers are among the most famous of our race from J.K. Rowling to Richard Branson to Stephen Hawking. It is the creative thinkers who not only create great works of art but also take science forward to great developments. Creative thinkers think beyond the norm towards cures for diseases, discoveries about our solar system, solutions to society's problems. Creative processes are essential life skills.

Sticking to a narrow curriculum restricts the chance to develop creative skills. Anything that your child does of their own volition will involve some creative thinking, whether it's building with Lego, playing with dolls or making dens; imaginative play; creating pictures and designs, models and sculptures, or any other unrecognisable heap of junk you would rather not have in your house; making music, designing a web page, singing, organising dramatic activities; dressing unconventionally, designing and customising clothes, experimenting with recipes, making films, exploring You-tube, using Warhammer and some computer games. Even bending rules. These are all valuable activities that develop creative processes. Children need lots of this type of activity to develop skills beyond the academic ones, for these are skills that will enhance their lives after their school years as much as qualifications will.

Most home educators like to give their children these opportunities as well as developing their academic skills. To do so they find that balance is the key. Balance between interest and necessity, the academic and the vocational, basic academic skills and life skills. And always keeping a balance between both the child's needs now and the need for that child to fit into the world later on.

Here are some simple everyday activities that we all pursue in our lives that you can involve children in. With discussion, observation and question-ing and shared decision-making as part of the activity, they encourage the development of life skills.

IN THE HOME

Cooking, preparing food, tidying and contributing to home maintenance, looking after pets, decorating, rearranging, general admin, budgeting, caring for others, gardening, family meal times, planning family activities, responsibility for own rooms, clothes, etc., recycling, pursuing hobbies, discussing a television programme, news or politics, using the computer or other devices.

OUTSIDE THE HOME

Shopping, visiting relatives, using and maintaining the car, using public transport, involvement with community activities, mixing in society, volunteering, fund-raising, library visits, sports, outings, holidays, visits to places of interest, travel, parties and celebrations.

If children are *involved* in daily life, rather than being entertained by the television or computer games all the time, they understand how daily life works. This is as much about the way we parent as the way we educate. Home educating parents can have a big impact on this part of children's education, and this is as much a part of their education as the academic study of isolated subjects. Home educating is a unique opportunity to address the need for this balance.

How to use curriculum and timetables to your advantage

To recap, here are some ways to get the best out of your use of curriculum and timetables:

- Use them as tools you can put down, or points of reference.
- Use them to help you reach specific goals.
- Use a curriculum that suits you – make your own if you wish.
- Discuss with others the way in which they use them.
- Continually strive for balance between academic skills, knowledge and practical life skills.
- Involve children in curriculum and timetable making.
- Involve your children in their education and the decision-making.
- Work to your child's needs rather than to the needs of a curriculum or timetable.
- Remain flexible. Change them as much as you need to. Constantly review.

- Never stick to them just for the sake of it.

- Don't forget you can adapt any curriculum to your requirements.

- Remember that neither a curriculum nor a timetable make an education; the *involvement of the learner* does.

Summary of the main points

- A curriculum is a pre-determined course of subjects or content usually aimed at moving the learner towards specific objectives.

- The National Curriculum is used in schools to standardise the content of what children learn and when.

- Home educators are not required by law to stick to the National Curriculum.

- Many home educators have a flexible approach to the use of curriculum based around their children's needs and interests.

- The use of curriculum and timetables and the practice of isolating subjects from one another are merely tools to help facilitate an education. They are not essential to an education in themselves.

- Many home educators make their own timetables to suit their children's learning preferences and their family circumstances.

- Home educators approach basic skills in a variety of ways, some through the use of graded workbooks, and others pursue them through their child's interests.

- Home educators have the choice of a wide range of other subjects, which can be based on the interests and strengths of the individual.

- Home educating is a unique opportunity to develop life skills alongside more academic skills.

Suggested websites

Department for Children, Schools and Families Standards Site: www.standards.dfes.gov.uk (type in National Curriculum)

www.direct.gov.uk and http://kids.direct.gov.uk (look at 'understanding the National Curriculum')

Parentscentre: www.parentscentre.gov.uk

John Holt and Growing without Schooling: www.holtgws.com

Chapter 6
What about Tests, Exams and Qualifications?

As with curriculum, home educators can make independent decisions about the tests, exams and qualifications their children take. There is an assumption that tests, exams and qualifications are essential for an education and are its only valuable outcome. However, this need not be the case. These too are tools and outcomes about which families can make choices. This chapter discusses this. It looks at:

What tests are for

What home educators use tests for

What exams and qualifications are for

How home educators choose exams and qualifications

Keeping the needs of the child at the forefront of decisions

The difference between qualification and education

Finding support for GCSEs

Making decisions about A levels and further education

Other opportunities and other qualifications

What tests are for

Contrary to what people generally believe, tests do not actually have a great deal of value to a learner. Rather than being an opportunity to learn something new, tests are to do with what *has been* learned. Therefore they are more about teachers gathering information than about a learner gaining new knowledge and skills. And the results of tests can sometimes lack accuracy and fail to identify the true needs of a learner.

The Standard Attainment Tests (SATs) were set as part of the National Curriculum in England to help measure children's achievement. They were supposed to be purely for the teacher's reference to help them better provide for their pupils' needs, and they were also supposed to be so unobtrusive that children were not aware of taking them and as such no disruption to the educational process. Anyone who has ever been involved with school will have quite a different view of SATs as being something very intrusive and highly stressful both for pupils and teachers (and parents) when it's time to take them.

This state has evolved because too much emphasis has been placed upon their importance. The tests are not actually important in themselves. What is important is the action that is taken as a result of them. If a test showed that a pupil appeared to be struggling then extra support could be arranged. Alternatively, those children who were high flyers could be identified and extra provision made to stretch them.

Sadly though, in many cases, SATs results are rarely used for this purpose. They have instead mostly become a means for unhealthy one-upmanship between pupils, parents, schools and league tables, and as such are more detrimental to the educational process than valuable. (Not to mention the waste of time spent in the preparation, sitting and marking of them.)

Tests are there to *enable* a learner, not ever to make a learner feel bad about their achievements. Since it is quite often the latter that is the result of tests, it is important to ask how useful are they really and what, when and how often do you want your child to be doing them? What, if anything, do they truly show, other than a performance on a particular day? Even the government is altering its position with regard to the value of SATs and constant testing.

Another thing to consider is that these tests support a *general* view of children; they make generalisations about what stage a child should have reached by a general age. As we have discussed children are rarely 'general'. Their progress and learning needs are all quite different. Therefore the results of general tests can sometimes be quite harmful to an *individual* learner.

Many parents are unaware of the fact that their children are not legally required to take SATs whether they are in school or not. Home educators are not legally required to take them either.

We probably all remember tests as part of our schooling and tend to associate them with education only out of habit, rarely questioning their validity. We remember things like spellings or table tests, or short class tests that tested a set of facts that we were required to learn. But although we might remember the tests I wonder how much of the content we remember and whether they served any learning purpose.

Tests for the purpose of coercing children into learning a particular body of knowledge, most particularly for a purpose they cannot see, can be limited in their value. They are more likely to make only a tiny minority of children feel good about themselves and leave the rest feeling inadequate. Self-testing, later on when children are revising for example, can be a useful tool to help learners retain knowledge for exams, but constant testing throughout their education is more likely to harm children's attitude than be valuable educationally.

The Cognitive Ability Tests (CATs), which children take when they first go to their second school at eleven plus, are a good example of the damage that can be done by test scores. These scores are supposed to indicate how well a child is going to perform during their SATs and GCSEs by the time they are 16. It is hard to imagine how anything so limited could indicate how a child will develop over the next five years accurately, knowing children as we do and how much they can change and develop during their teen years. What is more likely to happen is that both the learners and the people teaching them end up performing to that prediction, irrespective of personal changes in development. And many children are streamed inappropriately, are unable to rid themselves of early labelling, and never reach their potential as a result.

Tests that children undertake of their own volition, to test themselves, are different. Used like this, to reinforce memory or attain a personal goal, tests can be a more useful learning aid. The important thing to remember about tests is that they are simply that: another learning aid. And as such you might want to consider how much emphasis is placed upon them.

What home educators use tests for

Some home educators find testing useful to help them gauge their children's progress, to help them identify shortfalls, and to see whether their children's standard is abreast with children in school.

They find test papers on the Internet, in workbooks and in association with the curriculum or syllabus they might be using. Others devise their own informal tests and quizzes as part of their educational process; to give their children practice at doing them, cement learning, or as a fun way of learning.

Some home educators feel that tests are totally irrelevant to their child's education. Their children never take any until (possibly) they become relevant or useful to a particular outcome or set goal, perhaps if the child is taking exams by this stage. Other than that they do not do tests merely for the sake of doing them.

When thinking about whether you want testing to be part of your home education you might like to consider the following issues.

WHAT ARE YOU TESTING YOUR CHILDREN FOR?

In other words, what is to be gained and by whom? Sometimes home educators use tests to help them, as parents, judge how their children are progressing. They may do this for their own peace of mind, or to better enable them to help their children, or to measure their achievement against their peers in school. Some use them to identify whether a specific learning objective (like maths tables for instance) has been reached. Some use them to have a practice at an exam. Some children enjoy them and some families use them for fun. What is important is, rather than doing them for the sake of it or because other children are doing them, to have a *specific* and *clear objective* for using them, which is relevant to *your* child. This way they become a useful tool, rather than a time wasting chore where no one learns anything.

HOW RELIABLE IS THE RESULT OF A TEST IN TELLING YOU WHAT YOU WANT TO KNOW?

Test results only show how a child can perform at one particular moment in their life, so how accurate are they in measuring what you want to know? Tests vary enormously. For example, testing a times table could result in a child being able to tell you it today, but not a week later. Sitting a test paper for an exam needs practice at quite different skills: reading and interpreting a question; writing a coherent answer; working independently and to a time; having the knowledge of a subject – so what is it exactly that is being tested here? With different tests different skills are required and practised, which can be useful. But they are still only the *result of one performance* demonstrated in one particular way. A child might know all there is to know about food chains, but not be able to write it down. So what does a poor test result show: a lack of knowledge, or a lack of the skill to record it? And what sort of test is the best way to demonstrate knowledge? Would an oral discussion work better? Being clear about that at the start will help you decide whether testing is telling you what you want to know.

DOES YOUR CHILD NEED PRACTICE?

Some parents feel that tests throughout a child's life are a good preparation for tests later in life. Some parents feel that school tests bear no relation to later life. Other parents feel that school type tests too early in a child's life waste time with too much structured academic practice that is more likely to put children off learning, and prefer to give their child continued stimulating learning experiences rather than tests. Later on, when older children want to take exams, being prepared by sitting mocks is useful practice. But other than this you may want to question how valuable is continual testing in actually preparing children for real life, as few of us take many tests in later life and those taken are done so through our own choice and we find ways of practising for them (the driving theory test is a good example). What is most important, as we've already discussed, is to *keep learning pleasurable*. Whatever your purpose or intent it is best always to keep testing within that context.

DOES TESTING HAVE ANY INTRINSIC VALUE TO YOUR LEARNER?

If we are to keep our children's learning suitable to their needs it is important to ask how much testing is about the *child's* needs and how much it is more about *our adult* needs to have our children do them. Always question and be clear. Ask, is this helpful right now? And be aware of hidden messages that testing may be giving your child, like, learning is a boring chore and I'm useless! Or, tests are extremely stressful and unhappy experiences. They needn't be and indeed shouldn't be.

Testing is not essential to an education. But some find it a useful tool. As with all aspects of your child's learning, when using testing as a tool to facilitate it, always be clear about:

- your intention
- the purpose it serves
- your child's needs
- and keep an open mind about the results.

What exams and qualifications are for

Most parents tend to have a view that exam results and qualifications demonstrate that a person has reached a certain educational standard. Most people equate education with having qualifications. They feel that qualifications are what schools are for and qualifications get you a better life.

Parents and children have been encouraged to take this view increasingly as education has evolved. This is a point of view that we are all familiar with and most of us have no need to look beyond it. Parents are happy that their children are adequately educated if they come out of school with the qualifications they need to go to university or to find work. That is the purpose of their time in school. This view has served society well over past generations.

Society, though, is changing. Learning is changing and will change even more dramatically with use of the Internet. So this is quite a restrictive view of why we put our children through what we put them through sometimes, and what education, exams and qualifications are for and what they show.

Like test results, exam results and qualifications are assumed to be the proof of an education. Colleges and universities have traditionally required a certain number of qualifications to gain entry. Employers expect them. We all measure each other by them. We are all expected to obtain a certain number of GCSEs and A levels by a certain age and sadly we make judgements about people based around them.

It is true that for most people an educational qualification is a satisfying objective to work towards. It gives a sense of achievement. It enables learners to show to others, like colleges, universities and employers, that they have reached a standard. It is a useful outcome of study that we are all familiar with and an easy step to take to further education.

But there are other views to take on education, on qualifications and what they are for. And for the purpose of home educating it might be helpful to take a broader view, to re-examine some of our traditional assumptions and make informed choices about what part we want qualifications to play in our children's education, how useful they are, and be prepared to think around the way schooling conditions us to think.

Exam passes and qualifications are not a legal requirement of an education. They do not necessarily demonstrate that a person is educated in the broader sense of the word. They only represent a general academic standard and not whether a young person has a broader range of other skills, like social skills, application, personable skills, a broad intelligence and aptitude for work. Therefore it is also true that in some cases they are an inaccurate measurement of a person's intelligence. Consequently they are perhaps dated in the context of our contemporary and fast changing society, which requires fast changing application. Also, contrary to what schools lead parents to believe, there need be no time or age limit on when a learner may take them. A learner may take them when (and if) it suits their particular needs to do so.

Taking that broader view, some home educators are finding that there are other routes to college, university and work, once you look for them, that do not necessarily involve the traditional fistful of GCSE passes. So it begs the question: how valid are they in the context of a whole life and do other objectives and achievements serve an individual learner better?

It is from this wider perspective that many home educators make choices about exams and qualifications and what part they play in the education of their children.

At the age of 13 my son wanted to start his GCSEs and it was decided that he should study with the NEC doing a selection of GCSEs over a three year period, taking exams each year. This worked extremely well for him and he sat his first three GCSEs at 14, is taking two more this year and two more next year. Although he has not fully decided what he wants to do in life regarding a career, he does know that he wants to go to college to do his A levels at 16. So that's when the home education comes to a close for us.

Parent of two children, home educating for 11 years

How home educators choose exams and qualifications

Some home educators work towards educational qualifications in the traditional way. They feel this suits their family's need to have children with a traditional number of qualifications. This will always have been their intention and they gradually develop their children's skills towards this outcome. They want their children to have the same standard qualifications as children in schools and work towards that objective. The amount of qualifications and subjects studied varies from family to family.

Some home educators spread their study for qualifications over several years, perhaps starting younger and taking two at 14, two at 15, more as they mature. Some families base the number of qualifications they encourage their children to gain on a specific university entrance requirement, rather than studying for a huge number. Some encourage their children to study for them later, as suits their child.

Some families have teenagers who come out of school already having started working towards GCSEs, so they continue along that path working towards them in a traditional way, using study materials to help them.

Alternatively other families make different decisions about qualifications based on their educational philosophies. They take into account their children's wishes and interests, and how much importance they attach to qualifications within the perspective of the *whole* of their child's education and future intentions. These decisions are usually part of decisions that have been made throughout their children's education, which in turn are affected by how long the family has been home educating. It evolves as part of their ongoing education.

There are families, often those who have been home educating longer, who approach the education of their children as a life-long process that has a day-to-day value in itself, rather than simply a means to a qualification. So they provide an education suitable to their child's interests, needs and abilities at the time, rather than one that narrowly sticks to qualification as a need. This, they feel, keeps their children motivated to learn for learning's sake, rather than for the sake of a qualification, although qualifications may well eventually be part of that outcome.

Many home educators feel that when their children are clear about their own true objective and have an intention for themselves, then gaining qualifications presents no difficulty even for those who start this process much later than their school peers. It is the intrinsic purpose that gives them the motivation.

Home educating gives children and parents this kind of choice. In schools children have little choice about what route they want to take, or whether they even want to take qualifications or not. It is the element of personal choice that gives many home educated children the motivation they need to gain qualifications and most go on to do so successfully, even though it may be in a different time framework and a different range of subjects from those which would have been undertaken in school.

Many schoolchildren have little idea why they need to do ten GCSEs, for example, when the university of their choice only requires five. Obviously there is an element of competition involved, but home educating families are finding that their teenagers can still gain entry to universities with their five GCSEs (and even in some cases without them) because most of them demonstrate a wide variety of other life skills which some universities are beginning to value over masses of qualifications.

Some parents feel that children in school, particularly the more academic children, are pushed towards achieving high numbers of exam passes simply because it reflects well on the school tables. And it raises the question whether huge numbers of exam passes are of intrinsic value to the *individual learner*, especially if that learner has had no part in the decision-making process.

This brings us to the next section.

Keeping the needs of the child at the forefront of decisions

When children reach the age to be studying for qualifications they are of an age where they can have control over decision-making. Having control over decision-making is a way of respecting their wishes and fulfilling their needs.

It has already been mentioned how SATs do relatively little to enhance an individual's learning. SATs and school exams of a similar nature are usually for the benefit of staff. Their intention may well be to use the information gathered as a result to provide better for the student. But often this does not happen. Instead the results create labels and learners can become pigeonholed for life, often quite wrongly, by one moment's performance and have great difficulty stepping out of a set prediction. This is of no benefit whatsoever to the individual's learning process.

It is often the case that young children are labelled 'slow learners' simply because they were not ready for an academic style of learning at that stage in their lives. Poor test results are as much a demonstration of a child not being ready rather than concrete evidence that they are 'slow learners'. What those children needed was a different style of learning more suited to their particular needs. It may be one with more a practical approach, or with greater adult support, or it may be that the learner needed more time for personal development.

Whatever their need, home educating gives the option to meet that need *individually*, to see that individual learning progress is not inhibited by a general process that may suit other children, but which does not suit your individual. This is the way to make your child's own personal needs and rate of development part of the decision-making process when thinking about exams.

Discussion with the learner and giving them choice helps to achieve this. As children develop they can be introduced to the idea, through discussion, that they may one day want to do certain things, achieve certain goals and go off to college or university or find work, and to do so will need qualifications. Once they have reached the stage where they understand for themselves the benefits of studying for qualifications there is no need for them to be forced into doing so. They do it for themselves.

This learner-orientated approach to decision-making, rather than a traditional GCSE gathering approach, is a way of keeping children's needs paramount to decisions. It leads to greater motivation, higher achievement and heightened respect.

It is essential to remember also that each individual progresses at a different rate from another. For some children doing GCSEs at 16 works well. Others enjoy them at 14 or even younger. Some see no value in them at all. Some decide to do them much later. Some race through syllabi quickly. Others need extended periods of time.

Allowing each young person the right to be treated as an individual, irrespective of what others are doing, serves them best. When working towards qualifications, or not as the case may be, it helps to be clear about what is being worked for. That is, what part does qualification play in the *whole* education of your individual? Which brings us to look at the difference between qualification and education, discussed next.

The difference between qualification and education

In order to make thoughtful choices about taking GCSEs and other qualifications it helps to distinguish between something that many of us confuse. And that is the difference between qualification and education. We sometimes fail to distinguish the two. Identifying these as two separate outcomes for our children's learning will influence the learning we provide.

Some parents see education solely as a progression towards qualification. GCSEs and A levels are their sole intent for their children and are the only outcomes they are interested in, seeing those achievements as an end to education.

Some parents see their children's education as a more holistic process which incorporates a whole range of outcomes, not necessarily to do with qualification at the start of it, but which may well be a natural part of it in the longer-term. Their intention is based more on the ongoing development of an educated *person*, and is connected to the individual's stage at the time, and not focused solely on a future outcome.

*

Education is seen as *human* development, instead of qualification development.

*

Educating by taking care of the balanced development of a whole range of skills, placing as much emphasis on personal development as on academic development, provides children with many of those life skills they tend to lack when purely focusing on academic qualification.

Qualification is something to work towards as *part* of an education. But it is not the only purpose of it. And when qualification becomes the only thing deemed of value about an education it can become unbalanced. It creates a danger of destroying children's motivation and their love of learning, as it can make children feel that there is no purpose to their education *for them*. And perhaps there isn't. For there is no intrinsic purpose to pursuing an education that is not about the development of individual gifts and strengths, but rather is about proving to someone else what that individual can do, which after all is mostly what qualifications are all about.

Treating education as a holistic process with the individual at its heart and that individual's development as its sole intent recognises it as the life-enhancing opportunity that it is, of which qualifications may well be a part. Treating education merely as a means to qualification misses out on a wealth of personal development opportunities, most particularly the opportunity to make education an ongoing and valuable aspect of our whole lives. For qualification is not useful in itself, it is what you are able to do with it that matters and what you do with it is dependent on what other skills you have.

Recognising *education* as the objective, over and above qualification, will help to keep a balanced perspective when making decisions. Qualifications, for most, are a very important part of education. But they still are only a *part*. Each individual family has the freedom and the right to decide how big this part is going to be in relation to the whole of their learners' education.

Finding support for GCSEs

There are some guidelines for taking qualifications at home on the Education Otherwise website. With fast changes to policies these can quickly become out of date, as with any website, so always check sources.

When families have decided to do GCSEs at home they mostly resource their materials through the examining body they have chosen to study with. Their choice of examining body is made by the courses on offer and the location they choose to sit the exams. The Internet is the place to start this search. There is also a variety of GCSE course books in bookshops and you can order further study books through some of the publishers that produce them. Some families are opting for the IGCSEs or even the International

Baccalaureate, which some schools are now moving towards. It will probably be the case that fads for different qualifications will change as fast as society changes and this should be kept in mind when looking to the future.

Below are some websites that give information about taking qualifications and offer courses:

- www.qca.org.uk
- www.nec.ac.uk
- www.oxfordopenlearning.co.uk
- www.ccss.co.uk
- www.odlqc.org.uk
- www.aqa.org.uk
- www.ocr.org.uk
- www.edexel.org.uk
- www.sheffcol.ac.uk

It is a matter of trial and error to find which courses suit your family the best. Talking to other home educators who have pursued this route is always helpful to bring a balanced perspective.

Some families opt to do GCSEs at a later time than other children, as there are evening classes available for post 16-year-olds and other courses that incur no cost. Otherwise, home educators have to fund all exams and materials themselves. This is often why some families re-enter their children into school to study for their GCSEs or use their local college of further education. Many of these colleges now offer 14–16 programmes for children who want to choose alternative routes.

Making decisions about A levels and further education

By the time families have reached this stage in their education they usually have a particular goal in mind and are ready to aim for the higher level qualifications that will get them there.

This is often a time when students opt to go back into mainstream education, where facilities and resources are more readily available, but some families continue their study at home using distance learning courses. Some families opt to take GCSEs, AS and A levels alongside each other, for home education gives a mix of choices that are not available to students in school, and this is very much a time when students are making choices for themselves.

The choices children are given in school are very limited, and only choices within a given framework. Choices in schools are hampered by so many political, timetable and institutional influences they are not really free choices at all. Students educating out of school have greater opportunity to make free choices about which subjects suit them individually, rather than which subjects fit a school timetable.

There are options available to young people other than the traditional GCSE, A level, and university route once you look beyond the norm. Colleges of further education have a wider range of opportunities available to children who opt to take a different route and they are worth investigating. There is more emphasis in some of these courses on practical and vocational learning which suits many individuals better. Some colleges and universities offer access courses to students who do not have the standard qualifications. There is a new move to encourage parents and students to look at a wider range of qualifications beyond the traditional academic ones, which may be more suited to individual aptitude.

Other opportunities and other qualifications

When my son was 12 I was wondering how to provide qualifications at home and splashed out on a couple of NEC GCSE courses. I worked with him at first but he was uninspired and I felt it was a bit like school where he was being given work that was not interesting him at all and so was going in one ear and out the other. We gave up after a while and the folders gathered dust on the shelves.

At 13 he showed great interest in computers and so researched all the local courses and correspondence ones too which were very expensive. He found lots of free courses on the net and did these happily for fun. I did invest in one training CD but other than fun I don't think it was much help and as fast as things change in computers it was soon out of date.

At 14 we applied to the local college for an evening class, to get his 'foot in the door' the plan was. It was a very basic course (ECDL) and far below his capabilities but we felt they needed to see him in class and then if he reapplied for a full-time course later they would have seen him in action and would be less challenged by an early application. It did him the world of good as he was with adults in class which he enjoys, realised how much he knew compared to others, he got used to the college while it was quiet and had a taste of being back in the classroom.

> *When he was 15 he applied to do a BTEC evening course with them which they immediately said he could not do as he was underage. I pointed out he had studied with them before and they changed tack altogether and got a reference from a previous tutor which got him in.*
>
> *Now at 16 he is on a digital media course (National Diploma) which will provide work experience next year and can lead on to a degree course the following year. He also travels a bit now and has done volunteer work for years that has provided lots of interesting experience which I think looks good on a CV.*
>
> *He does not have any traditional GCSEs to his name but I think his selection of qualifications might be more eye catching to a future employer and he didn't have to slog away for two years or more providing essays and course work in subjects he did not enjoy. He has loved all his free time autonomously learning at home and seems to have all he needs to join the 'real world'!*
>
> Parent of two children, home educating for four years

Some families decide that academic qualifications are not what suits them at that particular time in their lives and find other opportunities for their young people. Many of the young people find them for themselves. They do voluntary work, work experience, find jobs, some use evening classes. There are often chances to further their study through work placements.

The Open University and Open College of the Arts offer qualifications for learners to study for at home. There is also an increasing range of more practical-based qualifications available to learners, like NVQ and BTEC, which suit many learners better than academic ones. These qualifications are increasing in status and giving students valuable practical and personal skills that some fail to achieve through the pursuit of academic qualifications. There are opportunities for combining and mixing qualifications to give the learners an approach which is suited specifically to them. The Qualifications and Curriculum Authority (QCA) website (see list at end of chapter) explains this in more detail. These courses can be accessed through local colleges of further education.

Home educators find that once they look outside of the traditional school qualification route there are other options that lead on to successful working lives as well as academic qualifications do.

Apart from our children's own choices of some geography, drawing, music and computer skills we basically concentrated on giving them a thorough grounding in maths and English. We did buy some maths and English Key Stage 3 books and found that these were more or less sufficient to take them up to what was expected at GCSE level. We also felt motivated to write and publish our own books for maths, English and science specifically with home educating families in mind (www.snailalley.co.uk).

...When our son was 16 and could leave (!) he did some part-time computer-related courses at a local college. A year later our daughter turned 16 and decided she wanted to get five GCSEs so that she could go into nursing. She enrolled on a one-year course at a local college...

...meanwhile we encouraged our son to also enrol on a course. Computers have always been his interest. He's always found reading, writing and spelling difficult. He was accepted on a BTEC course (equivalent to three A levels). The entry requirement was five GCSEs but he had no qualifications at all. He was accepted following a personal interview with the tutor on condition that if he wasn't making the grade in the first term he would be kicked off the course. He went from strength to strength, being voted student rep, winning the student of the year award and is now on the brink of going to university with offers from all the five that he applied to.

Parents of two children, home educating for nine years

Summary of the main points

- Tests are simply a learning tool and are not always of great value to a learner as they are limited in what they show.

- It is best to be cautious in the use of testing and be clear about your purpose in doing tests.

- Exams and qualifications are the traditional outcome of an education that we recognise but they are not necessarily the only valuable outcome.

- Qualifications are only a part of an education. Fulfilling the personal development needs of the individual is the most important part.

- Home educators can opt not to take GCSEs and other qualifications if they choose. Or they can choose to take them in a different timescale from that offered in schools.

- There are other routes available for students without GCSEs.

- There is a difference between education and qualification; identifying this difference helps the decision-making process.

- There are many websites available to help choose exam resources.

Suggested websites

Qualifications and Curriculum Authority: www.qca.org.uk

Open University: www.open.ac.uk

Open College of the Arts: www.oca-uk.com

Learndirect: www.learndirect.co.uk

Connexions Direct: www.connexions-direct.com

Chapter 7

What Is Life Like for a Home Educating Family?

This chapter attempts to illustrate the ordinary everyday life of home educating families and show how they cope and how, for many, home educating becomes the norm. It looks at:

How home educating families are the same as any other families, wanting the same things for their children

Typical daily routines among home educators

How home educators manage work

How parents cope with the children being at home full-time

Relationships within the family

The integration of real life and real learning

Coping with bad days and anxiety

Keeping a broad overview and positive perspective in the longer-term

How home educating families are the same as any other families, wanting the same things for their children

For anyone not home educating the idea of a family doing so is probably quite bizarre! And they probably think that home educators have a bizarre and very alternative family life. The reality is that home educating families are mostly very normal families who have just grown away from the school style of family life.

The range of families home educating is extremely broad. It encompasses families who home educate as part of an individual lifestyle they have chosen as an alternative to the norm and families who place huge emphasis on academic achievement and the recognised educational structure, who want to make sure their children achieve this through disciplined coaching and study towards that outcome, without the distractions found in schools. And in between these two extremes there is a whole scale of thousands of very ordinary families who are just doing the best they can for their children educationally, who just want the same simple things for their children that most parents want. For whether children are in school or not most parents still want the same things for them.

Most parents want their children to realise their potential, have their gifts and strengths recognised and their difficulties and weaknesses supported. They want their children to be comfortable and confident as they grow and have good relationships with a wide variety of people who are kind to them and do not bully them. They want to see their children blossom and develop their individual personalities. And they want their children to have the skills they need to move into a fulfilling future of work. And during this time, above all, they want their children to be happy.

Any parent who has given it any amount of thought would probably want these same simple things, but we generally don't often look that broadly, or beyond school. Home educating forces parents to consider these things in depth. And increasing numbers of families are finding that schools are not always developing these outcomes for their children, neither whilst they are in school, nor as part of their life afterwards.

So many ordinary parents are turning to home education. It is not parents who are elite, rich, alternative, academic or radical, although the home educating community has those among them, just as any community does. But it has a huge proportion of very ordinary families (without meaning to be insulting or derogatory in any way), just ordinary families who are taking the brave step to do something about the dissatisfaction they feel with the education schools are providing and the climate there. And although they may find themselves in a situation that is quite extraordinary to many, they are united with all parents in an ordinary aim:

✻

The welfare of their children, *educational and personal,*
both now and for the future.

✻

Understanding this common aim of all parents illustrates the sense of the ordinary in a situation that to some might appear to be quite the opposite. But as parents we are all the same in that we want our children to *thrive* and we want our children's *happiness to thrive* – this is every parent's bottom line whether home educating or not. This common aim illustrates how ordinary home educating families can be and how similar is their objective to that of non-home educators.

Typical daily routines among home educators

The typical daily routine for home educating families varies with their approach. Some have a recognisable school-style day with academic study between set times. Some have a study time in the morning and free time in the afternoon. Others have an approach where their study is integrated within the rest of the day and life's commitments, and learning takes place in a more spontaneous way.

Most families find that their routines alter as their children grow, their objectives change and the more experienced and confident they become with their children's learning. Each develops an individual pattern to fit in with their philosophies, educational goals and lifestyles and these patterns tend to evolve through trial and error. So perhaps there is no one typical routine any more than there is one typical family. And everyone's aim is to suit their individual learning styles and approaches and family life.

> We tend to do a couple of hours on formal stuff each weekday, but it still is a rather loose arrangement. Take today as an example. It's just gone 9 a.m. I'm waiting for the boiler people to ring giving me half an hour warning to get to my studio – they could ring anywhere between 8 and 6! So last night my son and I discussed what he could be getting on with if I'm not around, but we also know what we might do together. He is working on his personal statement for his college application – it's on the 'to finish' list for this week. That's how we work. More what we want to get done by a certain time rather than how much time we spend on work each day/week. It doesn't always work…we may have some days we have to put in a lot more time. Tomorrow we will get out for a walk and possibly do a bit of formal stuff together.
>
> As my son is 15, I don't need to organise other activities for him. He organises his own time. Perhaps I'm lucky in that he's not very interested in TV or

> *video games. He enjoys both, but has never been one to spend hours in front of a screen. He'll be messing about on piano or guitar, out seeing mates, sorting out music, etc. He cooks his own food, can sort out the shopping.*
>
> Parent, home educating one child for three years

A PERSONAL STORY

Home educating evolved into a way of life for us. Just like school was once a way of life full of early morning school runs, packed lunches, uniform and homework, home educating became a way of life with an early morning start for us parents when their dad goes off to work and I have a little time to catch up on my own work, household jobs and preparation for the day whilst the children get themselves sorted. Then we'd have time together for activities and studies in the morning with afternoons more likely for trips, visits, sports, socialising or personal pursuits and separate time. Some days we achieved loads, some days we achieved nothing. But I tried not to worry about this as that also happens in school! Integrated within the days were constant discussions, plans, physical activities and general life jobs that we considered as important a part of education as academic study, like providing ourselves with a nutritional diet, for example, and helping to prepare it. Television, computer and other techno-games were limited by time as we tried to keep a balance between activities, although I'm not saying I always achieved this! Balance between being in and being out, between sedentary and active pursuits. Late afternoon winding down towards supper, more snatched time for my work, and the children often having evening activities and clubs out of the house as other children would. This routine became as normal and everyday to us as school once was. We followed these routines more or less in 'term time' as school holidays were when their friends were more available for play and it gave us all a break from having to keep focused on education all the time. Although, when home educating, *life* became their education and as such not kept within set boundaries.

> We start our home educating day with a musical warm up: this is exercising and dancing to music. We then move on to about an hour of numeracy. This is done the old fashioned way, repeating the times tables, doing pages of fractions or whatever together. I have to do maths with my son this way because it is what works for him. We then move on to an hour's literacy without a break. This starts with him reading a page of the latest book we are reading to me... We then

move on to the next part of the lesson which could be language, creative writing or literary interpretation, depending on which day it is... Then depending what day it is we will move on to either history, geography or science. We will use the computer or an experiment pack for this. The time we finish is probably between 12 and 1 p.m., but then we are relaxed for the rest of the day. We might visit friends, go to the beach, go horse riding, sit by the fire and read ghost stories. There is no set agenda, it is whatever we want to do. Lots of times we just potter about and chat. Thursdays are different; there are no lessons at home. We go to the stables and he has a riding lesson, then we have sandwiches in the car and drive to his piano lesson. After that we go to the library and the old fashioned sweet shop and he looks in charity shops to see if he can pick up any old annuals. We then go to our family French class. Sometimes after that we stop in to see friends before driving the ten miles back.

Parent of one child, home educating for three and a half years

We currently have more of what I'd call a rhythm rather than structure. We make sure we go out every day at least once, more often twice, and also make full use of the garden for running off that energy. We do a lot of reading, we talk about themes that the children's interests have sparked, such as space, knights and insects. We cook, clean, tidy up. We listen to music and the radio, we watch a small amount of television, but that is regulated to avoid adverts and anything too manic. We do cutting and sticking, drawing and crafts and I generally try to keep things as calm and as fun as possible. I don't always succeed but at least the children know I'm human. My husband and both sets of grandparents as well as uncles and aunts are all actively involved in the children's lives as well as friends.

Parent of two children only just of school age, home educating since birth

A typical week for us is a bit like this. I am always up early, I grab the computer for a while and have a bit of a relax, then when I feel brave enough I get the teenagers up. My daughter gets up first but my son, well if it was up to him he would stay in bed till about two-ish, it's no good even thinking about doing anything until he is fully awake, so he normally wraps himself up in a blanket and plonks himself on the settee...then I try and get some writing done with my daughter and then she can choose what to do, all I say is that she must do some *writing about anything, some reading and some maths then she chooses the rest. She likes working on the computer. For my son it's skills for life stuff, so he might fill in a form that we grabbed from the post office, or learn about bills or making a phone call, finding out about train times, etc. He is also learning his theory for driving and does the hazard perception test online; he also helps my daughter to learn. I find that quite a skill to learn.*

On Mondays we usually go swimming with Education Otherwise (EO). Tuesdays are usually at home with shopping, cooking and some basic schoolish type work. Wednesdays and Thursdays we go somewhere and do a bit of English, etc.; sometimes someone has organised a trip (it is usually on a Wednesday or Thursday, and they have been on loads of educational trips, the last one was to a vegetable plot to learn about growing organic food and they had dinner made from everything out of the plot) and Fridays they have ice skating lessons with EO and we are there all day. Basically it's hard to fit in every bit of learning that we want to do, but it sort of somehow gets done.

Parent of two children, home educating for three and a half years

How home educators manage work

Home educating families fit their work around their lifestyle and approach to education.

For many families this means one parent working full-time out of the house whilst the other is with the children. This can be either parent. But it often means that one parent has to sacrifice their work. This is not always the case though. Some parents both continue to work, either job sharing, using flexible working hours or enlisting the support of relatives. Other families have a complete change in their working lifestyles, working from home, working part-time, integrating work or their own business within their home educating life.

There seems to be a variety of working lifestyles among home educators that are quite different from the traditional model, where families are finding other ways to accommodate both a working and a home educating life, making changes that only become apparent when they start to look for them. The Internet is changing the way we work, as it is changing the way we educate, and some families are making opportunities that they might have originally thought were impossible. Just as with broadening our concept of education, some families have broadened their concept of a working life, making it fit their home educating family life, like they once made school runs and child care fit their traditional working life.

As with all aspects of family life it can take some working out and working at. But there are often ways to be more flexible with a working life than the ways we are most familiar with, once we seek them out.

Some parents are very happy to sacrifice their working life to take the opportunity to home educate full-time. Some parents find they need stimuli that they found in work out of the house and to home educate full-time without that stimuli would be too challenging.

It is important that parents' desire to work and have other stimuli at times is addressed. In order to home educate successfully parents need to be as comfortable with their role as they make their children comfortable with theirs. This will probably mean compromise, negotiation and essentially communication between parents to see that everyone's needs are fulfilled, not only the children's. And whatever role is taken on at the outset can always be changed. Parents need to identify their priorities and consider their options. There are always choices, more particularly when you look outside the norm.

How parents cope with their children being at home full-time

Most parents find that there is no real problem with their children being at home full-time. But that is not to say it is not at times challenging!

Any parent, any teacher, or anyone who works with children full-time will endorse the fact that being with children 100 per cent of the time is an enormously demanding job. Perhaps most particularly because it is never simply one job; it is an enormity of jobs, a balance of multi-tasking and a demanding multi-role occupation. As with parenting pre-school children full-time, it is full on. To cope with it you need to manage not only your children's time and activities, but also your *own personal* time and activities.

✳

Creating personal time and activities is essential for parents.

✳

In families where there is one parent working full-time and the other home educating full-time with the children it is sometimes the hardest to find this personal time. When parents are job sharing, working from home or have more flexible working arrangements it can offer opportunities for each parent to obtain some relief from being with their children 100 per cent.

Creating personal time and activities for each person needs to be worked out for both parents. This can sometimes be challenging to fit into a life that already seems full with home educating/children/work, but it is possible. Here are a few things to consider:

- Look at *both* parents' lives, and consider the work at home with home education in the same light and having the same value as work outside the home earning. Make sure that both parents have time away from their respective work.

- When you are at home with the children full-time it will probably be the case that you have no need to 'educate' for that full day. Integrate personal time when you are 'out of bounds' within your home educating days.

- Explain to the children that sometimes parents need undisturbed time, just as children have undisturbed time when they might be watching their favourite programme, for example. Encourage *respect from* them of this time, as you demonstrate respect *for* them.

- Establishing your own time as part of your working day is a good routine to get into as early as possible and stick to it!

- Always plan *adult* activities for yourself as you would plan activities for your children.

- Do time swaps with other home educators.

- Meet with others informally where the children can be engaged on an activity without constant attention, like physical play centres for example, where you can have adult chat.

- Don't be afraid to 'pass' on a day occasionally. It won't hurt your child's education long-term if you give up and watch a Disney movie! It is more likely to harm your child's education if you get into loggerheads over something you're just not up to that day.

How you cope with home education will be based on what kind of relationship you have with your children. Home educating can often have a positive effect on that relationship and the next section talks about that a little more. However, there is one thing that is a major component of any relationship between any individuals whoever they are and whatever they are doing. And if that component is not present then it is unlikely that the relationship will be successful, happy, or endure.

That essential component is *respect.*

Asking for respect from your children and demonstrating respect to them helps keep relationships sweet. Sweet relationships make the difference to whether having your children around you all day is a pleasure or a pain.

For respect to work, it must be *mutual*. Parents have to command respect from the children by the way the parents *behave themselves*, and demonstrate respect to them by the way they behave *towards their children*. Children who have a model of respect around them understand what respect is and how to give it. Giving each other respect is a way of making living together easier. This can be as simple as always being courteous to each other, or more challenging like when you need to stick to your principles. It is important to speak, behave and act towards your children as you would like them to do for you. That's the *only* way it works. Above all respect should be consistent.

Relationships within the family

Just as home educating life routines evolve a little differently from school life routines, it can sometimes happen that relationships within home educating families evolve differently too.

When my son started school family evenings went out of the window. When he came home he didn't want to do anything except sit and watch the television. The (primary) school always gave quite a bit of homework, which he did not want to do. This was an absolute nightmare. I would be thinking 'Should I start it now and get it out of the way or should I leave it till later?' The problem was that because he did not want to do it we would be at it for ages and end up fighting. This makes him sound like a difficult child but that is the whole essence of my argument for why school does not suit all kids – my son is one of the easiest children going. He is sweet, cute, does not have temper tantrums and will fit in with almost anything you want to do. Then there was the trouble of the evening meal. My partner often does not get back from work until gone 7 o'clock and we eat about 7.30, this was too late for my son… We have never given him food at separate times but this seemed the only way. Then there was the worry of getting him to sleep so that he would be up for school. He's an owl, so I would be desperately trying to get him to sleep and I would fall asleep. I don't know if it's just our family but the evenings were no longer a chance for family life but seemed to be all about getting ready for school. Now we eat together and spend the evening together as a family. It is like a different life. I had got to the stage where I didn't enjoy the evenings at all. Now I really look forward to them.

Parent of one child, home educating for three and a half years

---

Many home educators have commented that the pressure that children feel from school creates many tensions that used to overflow into family relationships. Some have remarked on the changes not only of behaviour, but also in personality, of their young children once they started school. The tensions young children feel at school are bottled up until they get home and then released, causing unrecognisable behaviour patterns that had not been there before. Parents find that once home educating, those behavioural traits disappear and the child's personality becomes more familiar and there is less conflict between siblings. Some parents have also noticed that their relationships with their teenagers have improved when they have come out of school. It is easy to see how barriers can develop between parents and teenagers in school when both parties feel the pressures to fulfil the school's criteria for achievement. These demands have a huge overflow into family life.

Of course, there are many pressures with home educating. But parents and children have the choice to air views and concerns, have influence on decisions, compromise and work through difficulties thus keeping choices and communication open, an opportunity often not available to either parents or children in school. Keeping communication going between parents and children gives relationships the best opportunity to thrive. With home education there is far more opportunity to work on this.

Education becomes something that parents and children are working on together, rather than something that is done to children by adults, often in disrespectful ways. Once children understand this they are more willing to trust the adults involved rather than simply resist their suggestions. Trust helps develop good relationships.

If children, of whatever age, feel that adults are on their side, have something to offer other than nagging, offer them respect, are prepared to listen, are willing for the children to have some control over their activities, are willing to compromise rather than dictate, then children become more willing to compromise themselves, more respectful, more willing to listen, to develop responsibility for their education, and to see adults as people to help them rather than just something to rebel against.

All of this is based on communication. Communication is another key to successful relationships and is also based on respect. Communication in schools can be very one-sided and as such hardly communication at all. Home educating gives a better chance for balanced communication between parents and children, and consequently a greater chance for better relationships.

> *I feel I have a closer relationship than I may have done if they were in school. As we are together a lot we have time to 'experience' each other's moods and have time to discuss feelings and emotions.*
>
> Parent of three children, home educating for seven years

The integration of real life and real learning

Thus a home educating way of life becomes very much the norm for many families. The longer they home educate the more they find that life and learning are less distinct from each other. Education in schools creates a separation between life and learning whereas, in reality, if we look at our day-to-day lives, learning is going on there all the time.

A PERSONAL EXAMPLE

For example, at the weekend I learned to cook a new soup, experienced the differences in driving our new car as compared to the old one, learned about a new plant I bought for the garden. And today I learned a lot of new stuff about the Tudors I didn't know before from reading a story about Mary Queen of Scots to my daughter!

We all integrate the learning of new skills within our lives every day, sometimes without even noticing, and there is no reason why home education cannot be integrated in this way with everyday life. Many families find that it can be integrated quite successfully, and even when they are learning formal academic subjects. Integration of learning and life can be achieved by removing some of the school-style constraints which isolate learning, like the when, what and where, or placing less emphasis on them. When children realise that learning is a natural part of their everyday lives, then resentment of it diminishes.

> *It is our belief that learning occurs naturally at work and at play. The majority of our education is undertaken through everyday activities. We place a strong emphasis on visiting places of interest, making things and conducting experiments. Books, the Internet and television are used to reinforce these experiences, and as a substitute for activities we cannot undertake. Because our belief*

> *is that education is ongoing and involves the development of the whole person, we do not value testing and examinations, which tend to measure achievement in a narrow sphere of learning. When our children are old enough to know where their interests lie, they can choose to follow a more structured learning programme, if this is necessary to achieve a particular life objective.*
>
> Parent of three children, home educating for ten years

Integrating learning and life rather than keeping it separate helps children to see how it is part of what we all naturally do to develop personally and professionally, to develop a rich and fulfilling life, whatever age we are, whatever else we are doing in our lives, and wherever we may be. Learning, then, is for real life, rather than just for school and separate from real life.

Children rarely see this connection partly because of the physical separation of school and home. That physical separation, particularly in younger children, creates a mental separation. If they do not recognise learning as part of their real lives, their important lives, i.e. their lives at home, children can lose sight of the value in it and become resistant. If learning and life are indistinct from each other then this does not happen.

Many of the approaches discussed earlier in this book will help to integrate learning and life. With younger children this is perhaps easier as it is possibly part of the way we naturally parent; observing, discussing, questioning, creating, being physical, showing interest in the world around and our interaction with it. You also have their natural curiosity on your side.

With older children, if they've been in school and have that sense of separation, it is more difficult to break down any resistance they might have towards learning as something separate from their important lives. An approach where their learning evolves from their own interest, where they are listened to, where they have influence over decisions or make decisions for themselves, where they are involved in family life and living, planning their own activities and study time, creating their own lives and looking to their future, will help them re-establish the value of learning in their lives and see how the two integrate.

The closer that learning and life intermingle, the better attitude to learning will develop. The better attitude to learning the greater the opportunity is for learning how to enhance your own life with education. The more education enhances a life the more fulfilling that life will be.

Coping with bad days and anxiety

> *On days when it goes well it can be so rewarding and enjoyable, on dark and rainy days it can be pure hell. I have to remind myself that people who send their children to school also have days of pure hell!*
>
> Parent of two children, home educating for one year

A PERSONAL STORY

When I first started home educating all those years ago there were quite a few bad days and anxious days! I would like to say that there are not now, but I'm afraid that wouldn't be true. But what *is* true and rather comforting is the fact that *all* parents have bad days and anxious days *whether they are home educating or not*, whether they have children in school or not, children at university, or children flown the nest, however old they are. I had just as much anxiety about the children's education when they were in school. Bad days and anxious days are *not* exclusive to home educating and are *not* a result of it. Bad days and anxious days are part of the *parenting package* whatever your children are doing! I have also heard a saying among home educators: 'A bad day at home is better for the children than a bad day at school.'

> *Anxiety is part and parcel of home education: there are things I wish we hadn't done but we have all learned along the way. Having had six children we can see that they are all very different and needed various approaches. With that knowledge I am confident that they have done better at home than at school. Perhaps several of them would have had excellent results in 10 or 11 GCSEs, but at what cost? Just sitting five GCSEs each has been tedious enough and has taken up a lot of the 'free' time they would have used to follow their own interests.*
>
> *But anxiety is part and parcel of school education! When did you last have a conversation with a schooling friend where they said, 'Oh, his school is wonderful and the teachers are perfect and I can't fault the dinners...' I'm sure you see what I mean.*
>
> Parents of six children, home educating for 15 years

Bad days and anxious days are as natural a part of home educating as they are of parenting, and ways of coping with them are pretty similar too. Here are some suggestions:

- Contact with other home educating parents always helps. A problem shared is considerably eased.

- Don't be afraid to ask for advice. Even if it means ringing up someone from your contact list you don't really know.

- Choose carefully who you speak to. Develop a network of sympathetic parents who understand why you make the choices you do and are willing to support those choices.

- Look at *why* you are having a bad day or anxious day. Sometimes it's just a quick downer. Other times they might be happening regularly and you may need to change something…

- You might need to change your educational approach, or it may be that you personally need more time to regenerate your own energy.

- Home educating is a huge draw on your time, energy and personal resource, as parenting at home full-time can be. You need time for yourself; timetable that in too.

- Make sure you and the children are getting enough time apart.

- Put your anxiety in a wider perspective. Be realistic. Think in terms of: 'Okay, my child can't do this now…but I'm sure they'll be able to do it by the time they're 18!'

- If you are becoming frustrated over something you're trying to do with your child – leave it. Distraction works as well for parents as it does for children!

- Be realistic. Is your concern just a small storm that *seems* enormous but is nothing that a cup of tea and a break will fix?

- Bad days are often less about the children's education and more about nurturing yourself so that you can do it!

- Get out lots.

- Look after yourself!

- Make the decision not to think about it for two days then see how it looks!

Some days you just have to accept that you are not up to much that day and allow your children to occupy themselves. Console yourself that it would be the same in school. Teachers have their bad days too, when their teaching is uninspiring and little better than child minding. We are all human. And your child will learn a valuable skill from you in learning how to cope with bad days in their life.

As discussed above, keep realistic and keep perspective. All parents have days when their anxiety about their child's learning spirals out of perspective. Most particularly when they make comparisons with what children are doing in school. The reality is that:

✳

Every child is an individual.

✳

Home educating gives your child the opportunity to learn as an individual in an individual way. Unfortunately this does not necessarily give parents masses of ticks on tests sheets or conventional educational 'stuff' to show what's been achieved. But ticks on tests sheets don't really show that anyway, not for long.

One way to cope with sudden anxiety is to look at what's important:

- Ask if your child is generally *happy* – and no one could be every single minute.

- Ask if your child is gently *progressing* – it doesn't matter at what rate.

- Ask if your child is *achieving* things – it doesn't matter how small.

- Ask what it was like for them in school – whether you've *improved* on that.

I think the answers will probably put things back into perspective!

I think there will always be days of self-doubt, but even on a bad day things can be learned by looking at what's going wrong and trying to understand it. Mostly on our bad days we clip on the dog's lead, go to the river and she gets a really long walk. During that time frustrations are forgotten, the kids start to play again and if we're really lucky we might get to see a kingfisher!

Parent of three children, home educating for seven years

Keeping a broad overview and positive perspective in the longer-term

One of the best ways to help with niggling worries is to try and keep that broad overview. A view where you see your worries in relation to a wider picture of your child, what they've achieved, what you are trying to achieve, and an overall future objective that is more generic than specific. Many home educators find that anxieties and down days are often the result of focusing too intently on one small, specific issue. When they look at the wider view of the education and life their children are engaged in these doubts can be eased.

Home educating long-term is a long haul! It certainly feels like that at times, as many home educators would tell you. But it also gets better, gets easier the more you get used to it. And it is a fantastic achievement. But then so is climbing Mount Everest and not without its blisters!

However, when looking at that wider picture, these few years home educating are actually only one small part of a child's life. Looking at longer-term objectives, like well-rounded, happy individuals, as well as nearer educational objectives, like learning long division for example, keeps everything within proportion. For example, you could ask yourself: is the fact that my child cannot do long division now going to prevent them from having a happy and fulfilling life for ever after? And besides, will he not have another opportunity to learn long division?

Looking at it like this can even make some of our anxieties quite laughable! You can ask yourself all sorts of perspective balancing questions like these, throughout your home educating life. Questions like will this poor result now make a difference when my child is 30? What impact will not understanding Pythagoras' Theorem at this minute have on my child's future as a nurse? Does the fact that my child cannot write this story matter when he wants to be an archaeologist? And if you are worrying about those GCSE passes remember that they are not the only route to life ahead. Apparently, many parents now work in fields that have no relation to the degree they studied for.

Looking longer-term, expanding your overview, creates a balanced perspective and eases small clusters of worries that may become disproportionate to reality. It's a bit like when the children were toddlers and all we could focus on was potty training. I suspect they all would have managed it whether we worried or not. A few years down the line it seems rather insignificant, but you wouldn't guess that when we were making such a fuss about it and following them around asking if they wanted a wee every five minutes!

It also helps to remember your reasons for starting home educating in the first place, what benefits your child has as a result, and whether they would have had these benefits in school.

Home educating is a positive and life-enhancing approach to education that few children have the opportunity to experience; a positive and life-enhancing approach to life really. It is important not to let small learning hiccups cloud that wonderful opportunity. Home educating families have the opportunity to give their children a less pressured childhood, rather than a school-hood. That is a wonderful opportunity in itself.

Summary of the main points

- Home educating families have the same common aim for their children as non-home educating families: the happiness and welfare of their children, both personal and educational.

- Parents seek flexible ways to integrate their personal and working lives successfully with home educating.

- It is important that parents find ways to get recreational time and time away from their children for everyone's sanity!

- Good relationships are an important part of learning and fundamental to good relationships is respect.

- Parents find that one of the best approaches is to integrate learning with real life as much as possible.

- There will always be difficult days and parents find ways to help them cope with these times.

- Keeping an eye on the broader objectives helps to keep worries in perspective.

Suggested websites

There are many family sites and blogs linked through the main home educating sites already listed in previous chapters. These give personal insights into a home educating family life and it is worth exploring a range of them to get a balanced overview.

Chapter 8

What about Children with 'Learning Difficulties' or 'Special Needs'?

This chapter looks at:

The concept of 'difficulty' or 'special need'

How children with mild difficulties can sometimes thrive with a different learning approach and individual attention

How parents with special needs children approach home education

Where to find resources and support

The concept of 'difficulty' or 'special need'

Most of us like to think we're normal! That we can all learn normally and achieve what schools want us to achieve. And that anyone who can't has either a 'learning difficulty' or 'special need'. This is the normal view that most people adopt, and that we've been taught to adopt by the educational system. But there is another way of looking at it.

Instead of taking a black and white view of learners being either normal or not, achievers or underachievers, we could take the view that among us there is a wide spectrum of needs and that these are best represented on a sliding scale. The bulk of us probably fit somewhere in the centre of that scale which we tend to call the norm, and we manage to adapt our needs to fit into the kind of performance required of us in school. But the people who are further away from the centre of this scale, and those at the extremes who cannot, however hard they try, mould or adapt themselves to this norm are the ones that are called 'difficult' or 'special'.

However, the reality is more likely to be that actually many of us are fairly well removed from 'normal' or this centre, although we manage to cover it up and fit in. And the norm is in fact no more than another *generalisation* we make about children. When you think about it, children's responses in school may not necessarily be to do with learning, but to do with a host of other reasons.

For example, it might simply be that they don't want to be there and find it boring rather than them having a 'difficulty' with learning. It may be that reading is a pain for them and they hate writing. It might be that they are restless by nature and sitting learning in a passive way in a classroom is not the best approach for them.

In fact, it is far more likely to be the case that the things we require children to do to become educated, the place in which they are required to do it, and the way in which they are required to do it, just *does not suit their particular needs.* This would be a better view to take than automatically labelling those children who have no desire to cooperate with the school style approach as having a 'difficulty' with learning. For the 'difficulty' may well be with the approach, not with the child.

We could also approach the subject of learning from the point of view that we *all* have special needs. For in actual fact we all have learning needs that deserve to be addressed if we were all to receive equal amounts of attention. But unless these needs are drastically different from the norm and as such more noticeable, they seldom get the same attention as needs which are more noticeable or extreme. This is where an 'average' child can often go unrecognised as those who are more demanding receive unequal amounts of attention.

Approaching children as individuals, rather than from a generalised view where all children are expected to achieve the same things at the same time after being presented with it in the same way, will ensure that whatever those needs are, special or otherwise, they are more likely to be met.

There is no doubt that each of us has learning *differences*, however slight they may be. But these are not necessarily difficulties. *Learning differences only become a problem when we try and make all learners fit into a generalised view of how learning should take place and a generalised view of children.*

Changing the way we view this will help us to address our children's needs as individuals and get those needs met. As an example: think back to the outfit I described in Chapter 1 and how difficult it would be if the only outfit we could ever buy would be a size 16. If you were not a size 16 and you could not fit into that one available size of outfit, would you consider yourself to have 'difficulties' or 'special needs'? Or would you instead just realise that you needed a *different size outfit?* Similarly, with education, it could be argued that many children are not slow learners as they are made out to be; they just need a different style of education. And this is why it is so puzzling when you have a child who seems extremely intelligent yet is considered difficult.

We need to ask ourselves: why do we expect one style of education to fit all learners, when we do not expect one style of outfit to suit all human forms? The real problem is not with the learner, but with trying to devise an approach that suits their individual differences.

Although there are children whose needs are so particular that they need a very particular approach, many parents find that their children who were labelled in schools can sometimes thrive when home educated with an approach which suits them better and when they are released from school style pressures.

> All in all I'm very proud of the people our children seem to be growing into, and although I've definitely got more grey hairs and wrinkles than before we started on this road, I wouldn't have things any differently now. Both children are turning into a lovely mix of kindness and empathy, while being able to discuss and put forward their views and ideas assertively. Despite each having a specific learning difficulty, they have been able to maintain their self-esteem and confidence, something which I am certain would have been eroded had they remained in school. In so many ways we are moderate parents, but I feel pleased we were brave enough to take what, at the time, felt like a radical decision, and remove the children from school.
>
> Parent of two children, home educating for three years

How children with mild difficulties can sometimes thrive with a different learning approach and individual attention

We are all individuals. We are all different however normal we all are. We probably all see things in a slightly different way, like some of us see the colours blue or green differently, so we all learn slightly differently from one another, although some of these differences are so slight that they are hardly noticeable.

It is possibly the children who fall into these less noticeable categories who are the most badly let down. The group in the middle of the spectrum, the average, who fit in well, adapt well to school and the learning approach there, who behave and manage to learn appropriately if not dazzlingly. The children on the extreme of the spectrum get noticed and many get extra attention as their needs are diagnosed, but there is a huge group of children in the grey middle areas who do not fall into these categories who, because they are quiet and undemanding, may never get the attention they require to achieve their full potential. Home educating can change that.

Then there are those with more specific challenges to overcome, who struggle on silently perhaps wondering why they cannot manage to read at this point, wondering why they cannot comprehend algebra, or cannot sit still like everyone else does, when there seems to be no other explanation than believing they are just 'a bit thick', 'a bit disruptive' or 'downright naughty', as they are labelled by the professionals who are supposed to know about such things. This can apply equally to the 'average' child as it does to children with particular conditions, like Attention Deficit Hyperactivity Disorder, Asperger's Syndrome, dyslexia or others on the autistic spectrum. Many children get labels that they do not deserve, most particularly boys.

The fact is that few children are born 'a bit thick', 'a bit disruptive' or 'downright naughty'! Most are born with a well-functioning brain, a lively and enquiring mind, and an activeness and eagerness to be doing. Put these children in a school setting and these traits can suddenly appear to be 'difficulties'. So it is important to ask the question: is the difficulty with the child or with the school's provision?

As we've discussed throughout the book home educating gives parents a chance to educate their children not only as their needs require, but also to their true potential. Parents can create the kind of education that draws out their child rather than keeps them in specific confines: an education that takes into account their learning preferences and differences and works round them rather than make a difficulty out of them.

Rising to the challenge of providing for preferred learning styles their children have, rather than making their child fit styles that are clearly not appropriate for them, could make all the difference. And you can tell if a style is appropriate, for the child will be responding and learning.

To find the right approach we need to maintain a point of view that incorporates the ideas that:

- all children are different
- every child deserves to be treated as if they were special
- all children need to be treated with respect however they learn
- any learning problem may well be in the approach, rather than in the child.

A classic example of the last point is the way we approach learning for those children with dyslexia. Learning in schools and for most of us is something we traditionally associate with the printed word. For many children learning through the printed word *just does not work*. Not only does the child fail to learn from reading and writing, but also there is a danger the child will develop a sense of failure, resulting in low self-esteem and a continuing downward spiral of achievement.

As described earlier there are many, many approaches to educating, not just through reading and writing. Home educating is an opportunity to discover these other ways of presenting material and encouraging children to respond. When children are interacting with their education they are learning. When their response is resistant, either 'I can't do this' or 'I hate English', or dread, or procrastination, then probably the approach is not right for them and their education can be damaged, not to mention their confidence. Releasing children's learning from dependency on the printed word – and we have such image rich resources now with Internet, television, DVDs, etc., it is not difficult to do this – may transform a child's achievements and fulfil their right to have their learning needs properly attended to.

Other differences become clear in the way children concentrate or apply themselves, particularly to a more sedentary or second-hand style of learning where they are required to sit still for periods of time. Many children need active, practical, first-hand, experiential approaches that stimulate and engage them. Change the approach and some parents find that their child changes. Instead of disruptive behaviour, their child is switched on and engaged. Get the child engaged and learning is more likely to happen, even if it means fiddling with something in their hands while you explain. And many, many children need far more opportunity for outdoor activities than they get in school, whether it's through play, sport or field study. Being outdoors helps calm them, releases pent up energy, puts children in a lighter frame of mind which improves concentration, their overall cooperation and consequently their achievement.

Another difference in children that is often disregarded is their learning rate or speed. Some children have completely different development rates from their peers and do not blossom until much later. Some don't mature into reading and writing and understanding numbers until they are older. This does not mean that they are stupid or unintelligent. It means simply that their needs are different.

*

They are allowed to be different.

*

There is no law that says children all have to learn at the same rate. Most children usually get there in the end if they are not put off. And by the time they are 20 these different learning rates are hardly noticeable. It is schools that make learning rates important. With home education children need not be made to feel inadequate if they come to something later than others.

Individual learning approaches can break the boundaries of what we normally might do in connection with children's learning. And it is these diverse and alternative approaches that can make the difference between a child's progress being impaired and being made to feel they are a 'slow learner', or a child being allowed to blossom.

How parents with special needs children approach home education

Parents are equally allowed to home educate children with special needs, or particular learning differences, as they are any children. However children who have been statemented require special permission.

A statement of Special Educational Needs (SEN) is a diagnostic process that is designed to help make provision for those children who have extra needs in terms of their learning. It is usually done through school where parents or staff realise that a child may need specialist assistance. The statement then sets out special provision for those needs. Parents of children who are statemented through already being in school may still home educate, but they are required to satisfy the local authority that they are meeting these special requirements.

This statementing process is not imperative to the education of children with particular learning differences. In fact some parents of children in school find that it is not always valuable. There are few home educators who have not already undergone this statementing process through school who would opt to take it externally as in reality the provision made as a result is often poor and sometimes even unhelpful. Not every professional is in tune with a child in the way that the parents are. Parents are at liberty to make their own decisions about provision for their children.

Contact with others who have gone through similar decisions can be helpful and there are websites where support can be found. Some parents find that support organisations can be of real value when they have a child with specific needs, like those with dyslexia for example, or Asperger's, even if it is only the fact of finding a community of people who encounter similar problems. Sharing experiences often helps with coping.

As with all children, parents find that the most successful way to educate their special needs children is to keep their approach individual. To try and identify exactly what their children need – and this may be as much to do with their personal comfort and reassurance as it is to do with education – and to remain completely flexible.

*

A completely personalised education can turn a learning difficulty into a learning achievement.

*

Parents find it is essential to keep this open view rather than adopting a generalised view, listen to their intuition as much as professional advice, listen to their own child, work to a standard suitable for their child rather than all other children, seek out approaches that work for their own child rather than ones that work for other children. Essentially, start with the child and work from there, rather than starting with a scheme, approach or a system and forcing their child to fit.

Our son has Asperger's Syndrome (AS) and mild dyslexia. Presumably as a result of this, he was different in school and suffered a lot from bullies. With the school staff blaming him for provoking all the bullies, his confidence and self-esteem were non-existent. Rather than removing and dealing with gangs of bullies, our son was removed from the classroom and sat in an empty classroom. Eventually we decided that, even if we did a bad job of educating him ourselves, at least we were doing the job. Sitting in a classroom alone was not an education and our son was also extremely unhappy.

When we discussed this with him, he was so pleased to be coming out of an environment where he was literally living in fear. At the time, we didn't know that home education was legal. We just knew that, if we left him where he was, he might not live to school leaving age.

When we told the school, I believe they were just pleased to get rid of a problem so easily. They told us that he would never amount to anything because he was too easily provoked and would not concentrate.

We began by telling our son that his father and I said he must do English, mathematics and at least one science subject. We also said that, apart from this, we would help him to learn anything else he wanted to learn.

Our belief was that we could cover a broad range of topics within his interests. He was good at maths – no problems there; he chose to do physics as his science topic – again it was something he would have chosen to do anyway, and last but not least, he was seriously unhappy at having to do English but agreed that it was probably necessary for him in later life.

He decided that, in addition to this, he wanted to study volcanoes, the Second World War and the Romans in Britain…nowhere else…just in Britain! Bearing in mind we didn't know what we were doing was legal, we worked out that we could fit all this into each of the subjects he had been covering in school and we chose to learn British Sign Language as our language.

Our son is a great one for routine and he wanted a timetable. One of the things he had complained about in school was the number of times a set lesson changed, either due to staff absences or them trying to fit in something else which was required…but not time on the normal timetable. So we negotiated our timetable and agreed to try it for two weeks and, if it wasn't working, we'd renegotiate it.

To start with the English was first thing in the morning…to get it out of the way! Then it changed to the afternoon…when he was awake! Then it was just before lunch…because he didn't like it anywhere else!

Various other lessons changed around as well; there were five or six 'renegotiations' until we had something we were both happy with. The timetable also included going shopping, housekeeping and cooking. This had to be included because he'd been promised 'no surprise changes'.

My first task was to establish what he knew. Theoretically, he knew all that the other children his age knew; he'd been to school and had an excellent attendance record. I bought a load of revision guides from CGP Books for his age and I went through them with him saying 'I know this' or 'I've never done that'. For those things he said he knew, I gave him some work to do on them and if he could do it, we moved on. If he couldn't, or it was something he said from the outset he didn't know, I'd go to the very foundation and we'd sail through the beginnings but it allowed me to see exactly where I needed to start from.

This turned out to be useful as it also allowed me to learn that he did have concentration problems as well as memory problems, both of these being very common with AS and with dyslexia. I also learned how long was right for his concentration levels.

I'd read a lot on American home education sites about themed learning, so I thought we'd try that as it sounded interesting. We started off with the Romans and did collage and art work on triremes and mosaics; we did Roman numerals in maths; we did some cooking according to books from the library and geography was where the Roman towns were in Britain and what they're called now. It wasn't a success! Although I had separated it out into separate bits and thought that saturation was a better learning tool, I was wrong. From his point of view, we spent all day doing the Romans. He couldn't differentiate between the different bits. Scratch the themed learning!

So, geography became the volcano study...but starting back with Pangea and plate tectonics. History was the Second World War. Physics was kits from Opitec. Maths was the CGP books and cooking, decorating his bedroom and deciding how big a skip we needed to clear the front garden. English was us sharing all the parts in Romeo and Juliet and reading the play between us, watching it on a video from the library and watching West Side Story. There are loads of websites for those learning English as a second language and they all do worksheets on specific language areas. These were very useful as they were not aimed at babies and felt older and more suitable.

During this time, we only left the house to go shopping. He was terrified of being out and meeting any of the children who'd bullied him in school. We were only allowed to do the shopping when they were in school. I remember a Teaching Day when we went to the supermarket and there was a gang of lads there; we had to come straight home again.

This lack of confidence showed up in his learning as well. Everything was 'I can't do this'. I always agreed with him. He was right. He couldn't do it...yet! It became very important to do things in tiny chunks with very small goals. We needed positive reinforcement all the time. It also meant teaching him to cope with his own learning difficulties.

He found it very frustrating to learn a maths concept one day and, the following day, not know how to do it. It was more demoralising for him as he remembered learning it the day before. We developed the routine of spending ten minutes revising how to do something and then move on to revising something else and then ten minutes doing something new. So, for example, on Friday for maths, we'd spend ten minutes on what we did new on Monday, ten minutes of Tuesday's new thing, ten minutes of Wednesday's and Thursday's and then we'd do ten minutes of something new. I explained to him that, because of the AS and dyslexia, he had short-term memory problems. By repeating things, I told him we were getting it into long-term. However valid that was, or was not, it was an explanation that he understood, that allowed him to work with it and to learn and gain confidence that it would only take time. That it was 'his' style of *learning. Not that it was wrong… just different to how a lot of other children had learned in school.*

As he grew more confident, his learning became easier and he didn't need so many of the revisions. He was starting from an 'I can do it' standpoint. It's amazing the difference that made.

We'd been home educating him for nearly two years before he would leave the house easily. At that time a major renegotiation of the timetable took place. He was nearly 13 years old at this point and we felt he needed to learn to cope with change. It was surprisingly easy. We put a slot in the timetable which was 'unplanned activity'. This led to trips out and finally meeting up with other home educators.

He'd also grown beyond my ability with physics and, with his dad working full-time, he couldn't fill in. Our timetable was not allowed to go into the evenings when dad was home. So, we had a tutor for physics; initially an hour a week and then two hours a week.

All other subjects were done with me. Either I already knew it, I'd have read up about it the night before, or we learned it together. There were a couple of areas of maths that I couldn't get the hang of; he needed them for the GCSE he wanted to take and wouldn't have another tutor. So we paid his physics tutor to come in for a couple of extra hours to teach me and then I passed it on.

We stopped 'full-time' home educating when he was 16 and he achieved four GCSEs, but we assisted his learning in college where he did A level physics and AS maths. He then went on to do an ONC in Electrical and Electronic Engineering. He achieved distinctions in his results and was put forward for the Young Achiever of the Year Award. Finally he did a HNC on a day release from work.

Parent of one child, home educating for seven years

Where to find resources and support

Some of the home education organisations, like Education Otherwise, have special contacts that you can ring for particular support. It is always helpful to talk to others, for support, and to keep your own concerns in a wider perspective.

There are also increasing numbers of organisations and websites to support particular conditions as they become more widely recognised and known. Below are some to investigate. Also try the government and parent websites listed in previous chapters and the BBC website.

Our son had previously been diagnosed with dyspraxia but he obviously had other challenges too as he found it hard to mix with others and couldn't understand why people did what they did. He had major temper tantrums and he didn't play like other children but also seemed very intelligent and mature.

Day one of home education was such a relief, we felt like we had got the 'get out of jail free' card…our son didn't have any more tantrums, no more days wondering why he is having a fit about something that we didn't understand because now we knew exactly what he had been doing. He could now eat when he was hungry and we realised that his blood sugar levels were all over the place due to stress no doubt and having access to machines full of chocolate and fizzy drinks. Also we found out later he had not been able to cope with the noise in the dinner hall so hadn't tried to get any lunch.

His sleeping was very unsettled at first as he didn't really believe he was not going back to school and dreaded waking up one day and being told he would have to go back. Even when we repeatedly reassured him he still did not feel safe. Each day he told us more of the things that had happened at school; he had not been able to get the words out when he had been so stressed with it all. He also started having nightmares about what went on at school – it was like he was going through some kind of post-traumatic stress syndrome. But as he didn't have to get up early it didn't matter so much that he couldn't get to sleep until 4 a.m. and so could, and often still does, lay in to lunchtime.

Gradually he recovered and trusted that this was it and that he was free to be himself and could relax. With this came eager learning, a driving force in him to discover all those things that he had never had time to research and learn about. He has taught himself a huge amount and is extremely confident in many areas that he hopes to follow through for future employment…but what he has learned the most is that he can be happy.

To anyone who is daunted by the idea of taking responsibility for the education of their child, especially a child with special needs, I would say just do it and see how you get on. The pleasure we have all gained from having our son at home learning with us is a part of his life we would not have missed for the world. In my opinion he is far more prepared to step out into the world than his classmates are. All our children are different and deserve to be given an individual way to live and learn that suits their needs. I am so glad we had the opportunity to do this with him as we have learned so much about ourselves too.

Parent, home educating one child for four and a half years

Summary of the main points

- We all have different learning needs, however slight, or extreme, or special, which deserve to be addressed.

- Some of these learning differences only become a problem when we try and make all children fit into a generalised view of learning.

- Children may not be 'slow learners' at all. They may simply need a different approach to learning.

- Changing the approach can make the difference between failure and achievement.

- A child's need for a different approach is not a sign of limited intelligence or inability to learn.

- Keeping the approach particular to the individual child is the best way to tackle learning.

- It is important to start with the child and work from there, rather than start with a system and make the child fit.

Suggested websites

National Attention Deficit Disorder Information and Support Service: www.addiss.co.uk

Nasen (formerly the National Association for Special Educational Needs): www.nasen.org.uk

Home Education in the UK – Special Educational Needs: www.he-special.org.uk

Dyslexia Action: www.dyslexiaaction.org.uk

National Autistic Society: www.nas.org.uk

Independent Panel for Special Education Advice: www.ipsea.org.uk

Advisory Centre for Education: www.ace-ed.org.uk

Tinsley House Clinic: www.tinsleyhouseclinic.co.uk

Chapter 9

Where Do Home Educated Families End Up?

This chapter looks at:

Some home educated children and what they are doing now

Children returning to mainstream education

What parents might want for their children both short-term and long-term

What children might want and discussing it together

Differing views on education, what it is and what it's for

What parents might consider success to be

How to keep an open view and an individual view that relates to the child

Educating for intrinsic value rather than for outcome

In the end

Some home educated children and what they are doing now

I have never been to school and have been taught at home in some way or another since I was two. My parents didn't like the school system and were looking for alternatives – this was it! In all of the years I've been home educated I have always been given the option to start going to school, but I never liked the idea of changing my life to that degree and being home taught was what I was used to. My earliest memories of learning were the 'Peter and Jane' reading books; I loved learning to read and each new lesson with my mum on a new set of words or sounds was exciting at the time. The only 'real' subjects I remember doing with my mum at the start were maths, English and French… I set my own timetables now and do the right amount of work when I need to – most of the time. I'll be starting college next year; that'll be a new start in my life and an end to my home education.

As for socialising, I had a sparse social life at first consisting of routine meetings of various people. I have always been involved with EO groups and have had a lot of fun and made a lot of friends from them. As well as these, I have always made use of local sports, social and hobby clubs to meet new people. I think home education has made it easier for me to mould myself into an individual and made me more resilient to the pressures of conformity that I would get if I went to school. I think I would have more friends if I went to school, but this is unimportant to me. Thanks to home education I know who I am, what I can do and what I need to do – I'm glad I never went to school!

Student, home educated since the age of two

Our oldest children all took four or five GCSEs from home and then went to local colleges.

Our 21-year-old has been in full-time employment since A levels while studying for a maths degree with the Open University. He had no desire to go to university after two years at a sixth form college ('I've had enough of education for now'), and has been much happier with the OU both with the study techniques and the fees!

After A levels our 19-year-old spent a year in China learning Mandarin and is now back in the UK, working while studying for an international-focused degree with the OU. He has looked at universities but is also not happy about the time wasted there waiting between lectures.

Our 16-year-old is taking maths, dance and music A levels at a local sixth form college.

Two of them are fairly confident that they would home educate their own children depending on their spouse.

All of them have found their main issue with education at college to be wasted time – waiting for others to arrive/be quiet/get off their phones, teacher being absent, constantly redrafting coursework, waiting for help from teachers. They'd rather do it themselves.

Parents of six children, home educating for 15 years

Children returning to mainstream education

Many families continue with home education right through their children's school years. Other families opt to return to mainstream education. Reasons vary from family to family.

Some families have personal circumstances that prevent them from continuing to home educate. Some find that home education does not work for them. Others find that a period of time out of school being home educated is enough to overcome difficulties and they settle back into school more happily as a consequence. Some families have children who are inquisitive about school if they've never been and want to try it out. Some children want a bigger peer group around them as they get older. Some families use schools later for exam support or other specific educational reasons, obtaining qualifications for example. Other families use colleges of further education for this purpose and take advantage of the 14–16 courses now available to teenagers who do not want to be in school.

It is perfectly possible for children to adapt between home and school, even though there are obvious differences in provision, and most children go on to do so successfully. The way to help this transition is through keeping open communication between all parties, listening to the child's concerns, keeping the child's needs and wishes as the basis for decisions. Children are very adaptable and accepting. They cope far better with change than many adults. If the child is part of the decision-making process they feel respected and are better able to adapt.

Although there may be a difference in what they know and what they can do, home educated children are usually well able to integrate and succeed when they return to school or mainstream education. Often, if the option for them to leave again if necessary is open to them, they are better able to cope with circumstances that may have once seemed intolerable.

When my children were 11 years old, having been at secondary school for only three months, my son wanted to be home educated. I have always considered my children's well-being and state of mind far more important than learning history dates or algebra! I could see that this was the best thing for him at the time. He was much calmer once he was at home, we were doing all kinds of things, a bit of school work from the books I had bought, but also lots of talking about life, things we wouldn't have the time to talk about normally because of school hours, homework and finding time for them to be with friends. We would visit somewhere of interest several times a week.

His sister saw the benefits and joined us a couple of months later. We all really enjoyed the experience. The children found the break from the 'madness' of school very beneficial. Although I was really worried about the prospect, we have always been very close, and it turned into a further bonding experience between us all. We joined the local home educating group and enjoyed attending events and receiving support from each other. In the evenings and weekends the children would spend time with the children they would normally see at school.

After about a year and a house move they both decided they wanted to go back into school. They felt stronger and more equipped to deal with the 'madness' school has to offer. They settled back in and have been there for a couple of years.

Single parent of three children, two home educated for one year

I started home educating over ten years ago now after my eldest son was bullied in the first year at primary school. We began by attempting to replicate school, sitting at a table in the mornings and concentrating on outings and sport in the afternoons. That formality didn't last long but having them at home worked very well, especially as my husband worked shifts including many weekends, so would not have seen so much of them if they had been at school. Our other three children joined in and we were able to do lots of things together, especially sports and trips. The boys went to secondary school at 11, my elder daughter at almost ten went to primary school and loved it. They couldn't praise her highly enough, intelligence and character.

Now I have one eight-year-old daughter happy to be at home.

Parent of four children, home educating for ten years

Some children stay in school for a short while and then come out again whereas others are happy to continue their education in school and get what they want from it.

There is, however, no specific requirement for children to go back into mainstream education at all if they do not want to and home education is working well for the family. Some children are home educated throughout.

They successfully get where they want to go or gain qualifications they want without *ever* having been in mainstream education.

What parents might want for their children both short-term and long-term

Most of us are ambitious for our children whether home educating or not. We all have that rosy image of them either collecting their degree or happily earning their millions. Most of all we want them to be successful. But we perhaps do not look much beyond that traditional academic definition of success when we are thinking about what is best for our children now, over the next few years, and in the long-term.

We perhaps need to think it through more carefully, perhaps more specifically in relation to our individual children, rather than in relation to what a mass of other children are doing, and more honestly.

With honesty in mind, here are a couple of thought-provoking questions for you to ask yourself while you are thinking:

- Is what you want educationally for your children more for your sake, rather than for theirs, if you are brutally honest?

- Which is your highest priority: academic success or happiness or fulfilment?

We probably all have a reactive answer to these questions straight away. However, what most of us need to do is not stop at our first reactions, but to keep thinking. Keep being honest beyond those first reactions and keep questioning. For there may well be rather a lot that we urge our children to be ambitious towards that is as much for our own comfort and peace of mind, personal parenting satisfaction, to ease our own worries, or even social one-upmanship, as it is for the personal development of our children's lives, either now or in their future.

We might also find that success and happiness and fulfilment are so tied up with one another as to be indistinguishable. So perhaps just pushing for success, as in academic terms or high income, is no use without defining exactly what you consider success to be if it does not include happiness and fulfilment, and in turn what those two elements might consist of in themselves.

The answers to these questions give us something to truly work towards when we are making provision for our children's education and when we are providing for their individual needs.

Children who have particular interests, strengths or ambitions for themselves are the easiest to cater for. I know home educated children who, from a very young age, seemed to be going in a particular direction or who had talents and interests so strong that their purpose was quite clear. For the parents it was just a matter of providing for these interests and maintaining a healthy balance of other skills, subjects and experiences along with them.

For children who are not like that, probably most of them, it is much more difficult to see where you are going with your child's education other than providing them with the basic skills and experiences all children would have and constantly presenting new stimuli in the hope that some direction will come when you hit upon the key.

It is also very much a matter of trust.

Many children do not find their direction until much later in life so it is impossible to be educating towards a specific career path. Unfortunately, this is when many children are pushed towards academic outcomes only and many other more creative experiences are neglected. It seems rather bizarre for children in school to be making decisions about options for the rest of their life so young, when they can have no concept of how that life is going to shape up.

What you could do instead is look to the experiences you provide for your children day to day, keep them varied and balanced, and keep them pertinent to the child *at the time* rather than solely working towards long-term, isolated academic outcomes like exam passes. Obviously we all want to plan longer-term, but it is important to keep that in the perspective of the fact that no one can accurately predict the future.

Finding the balance between educating for now and educating for the future is possibly the only valuable option until a purpose or direction that is intrinsic to the child is reached. And also create a balance between what you feel your child will need, and what the child themselves might want.

What children might want and discussing it together

We all know that small children are egocentric little beings. They are totally absorbed in their own little world and it is difficult for them to see any kind of reason other than 'I don't want to'.

But they do change. And they do see reason eventually when we continually discuss things with them; discuss the world they see and how they fit into that world, what the world can do for them in return for the things they do. And this is how the activities the children want to do, and activities parents want them to do, can be negotiated. Explanation, discussion and giving them the 'why' for the things that happen helps them see beyond their egocentric little worlds.

Anything we ask of them should be backed up with a reason. Not only is this a part of respectful relationships but also, if they have been given the reason for the things we ask, they are more likely to build a wider understanding and become more cooperative. All through their education, even when they are quite young, they deserve to be given a reason, and it is only fair that we should justify our own actions. They need reasons that are relevant to real life. As they get older they see that the reasons we give them relate to our adult life and they soon begin to understand that the things they most want in their adult lives can most often be acquired through education of one sort or another, certainly through their own input, action and efforts.

Saying 'you need to do this maths now because sometime in the future you might need a GCSE' will not be as valuable a reason to a child as something more like 'understanding numbers and how they work helps us budget and save for the things we want' for example, depending on the age of the child. This way our reasons are directly related to life.

We also need to make our children feel that not only do we ask that they cooperate with us sometimes, without perhaps understanding the reason, but that we cooperate with them. To do that we need to listen, listen to their chat and their reasons, see how their wants can be fitted into their education, be prepared for negotiation and compromise. When children feel their desires are considered and respected they are much more open to reason, as indeed I am when I am listened to.

Education is not about children answering the needs of parents to have kids with high IQs or more qualifications than the children next door. Education is purely for the self-enhancement of the individual. And that individual's desires need to be allowed to play a part. For their desires, their wants, their gifts and strengths are what make up that individual and if they are not taken into consideration then education cannot be about their needs at all. It becomes only about parental and adult needs.

Obviously, young children do not know everything. They sometimes do not even know what they want. Part of educating them is to help them know what they want, rather than just to do stuff to please the adults around them. Help them understand what makes them feel good, what they enjoy, what they are good at, how this fits in with the world and what they might want from it, like work for example. And these important discoveries are an intrinsic and highly essential part of their education if they are being educated towards a fulfilling life. Once they understand the relationship between themselves and the wider world they are truly becoming educated and will be ready to make decisions about their future themselves.

Education needs to take account of children's wants, desires and interests, in balance with practising academic skills, if it is to be intrinsic or relevant to the individual. Home educating gives parents a chance to maintain a balance. The priority you want to give to these will depend on your educational view.

Differing views on education, what it is and what it's for

There is no doubt that home educating forces parents to think very hard about education and what it is exactly.

I suspect that most of us initially thought about education as schools teaching children what they need to get qualifications and once children get those qualifications then they are educated. Throughout this book I hope I have introduced a broader idea of what education might be and how, in most cases, this broader view better enhances the development of a rounded and fulfilled person.

Many parents who home educate begin to discover and build their own personal view of education that expands beyond our traditional views. One parent described his son's education to me as being for the purpose of understanding the world around him and how he relates to that world. This view is based on a wide perspective of education as something that continues to increase understanding and skills throughout life. It has no boundaries in terms of time, place, beginning and end. It has no relation to the idea of education that some parents have as something to be 'got'.

The view of education as something to be 'got', like a commodity, immediately puts it in the context of once got, there it ends, which is an extremely limiting view and not one that could extend to the idea of education being a life-long, life-enhancing process that leads to a better chance of fulfilment.

Some views of education also involve the idea of teachers and teaching needed to aid this 'getting an education' model. As we've discussed, teaching need not be part of a definition of education, nor teachers essential to it even if at times they have their uses. Teachers and teaching were originally needed because most people did not have either skills or knowledge or resources to learn for themselves. That is no longer the situation today. Today nearly everyone has access to knowledge and skills they might want to learn for themselves. So teachers and schools are not as essential for people to learn in the way they once were, even though there is clearly a role for encouraging, stimulating and providing support.

The word education comes from the Latin *educare*, which means to bring out or lead forth. This is a complete reversal of many people's more common view of education as a filling up process, which sees children as vacant until they are so filled up. Schools tend to take this common view and are indeed filling our children up. But sadly during this process little leading out takes place of anything that might already be there, little recognition of the fact that children have many inherent qualities, interests and desires. These are mostly neglected and disrespected in the pursuit of this 'filling up' with prescribed syllabi for the purpose of academic attainment.

Measurable academic achievement makes schools look good. It makes politicians look as though they are making the right policies and therefore gains them votes. Prescribed syllabi can be delivered to masses of children by few adults thus costing less. But the trouble is that academic study suits only a small percentage of our children and it is only a small part of an education. And there is always a major flaw in prescribed policies:

*

Prescribed policies usually neglect individual qualities.

Prescriptive educational processes usually fail to equip children for the individual lives they are going to lead.

*

The wide variety of children in the world, the diversity of personalities and backgrounds, the way in which we now parent and respect our children and young people and provide for them, has totally outgrown our traditional model of a prescribed education as something to be got.

We now respect children's rights and freedoms, we have immediately accessible information available to all, and children are dramatically different from when our current educational system was set up, so we need to ask what sort of education would serve these new aspects of our society best? What view or model of education will serve to engage and stimulate the young people of today who are brought up in this more liberating way, equip them to live their lives in this fast and constantly changing society, develop in them a sense of respect and responsibility, esteem and fulfilment with their place in that society and with their work?

We've radically changed our view of raising children over the past 50 years. But we've hardly changed our approach to educating them, or their position in that education, or the outcomes of it.

If we look at it honestly children have always been regarded, and treated in schools, as an underclass. As an underclass they have no choice but to suffer the impositions our style of schools and becoming educated has put upon them. School, for the most part, disempowers children in order to control them and continue with our adult stance of filling them up with what we adults deem to be a suitable education.

As our society has developed we have encouraged children to move away from this position as an underclass and given more respect to their wishes and listened to them. We have encouraged them to have voices, increasingly led them to be independent and adult very early in relation to what they once were. Yet we still expect them to tolerate lack of choice and freedoms, and sometimes abusive circumstances, whilst we try and educate them. Then we wonder why there is truancy, rebellion and children without basic skills.

It is surely obvious that if we got education and schools right for our children then there would be no truancy. If schools were good places to be where children were treated well and education exciting then there would be relatively no rebellion and few children without basic skills.

I do not know any home educated children without basic skills. It is relatively simple to develop basic skills in children as long as they are not put off education, as so many are by schooling.

But home education is not a complete answer to the problem some have with schooling in this country. The answer instead lies in changing. Changing our view of education; how it is made available to our young people; their understanding of what it can do for them and thus what it is for. And it is the parents who can have the impact on changing this, not the politicians. As parents we need to be clear about what our view of education is and what it's for in relation to our world now and our children now, not 50 years ago.

So what is it for? If it is not just for qualification and as something to be got, what instead might be an outcome or purpose for being educated?

When we think about education we tend to look at what our own particular child is going to get out of it. But actually, the impact of their education is not confined solely to them. Each and every one of our children is part of a whole society. And each one of our children is going to have their own impact on that society. Each of our children is going to make a difference.

That may be quite hard to believe, but just consider it a moment. We generally only tend to consider the people who make a noticeable difference like Stephen Hawking, for instance, or Richard Branson. But even less famous people, who seem insignificant, can make a difference. Even one small gesture of help or friendship, support or service to another human being makes a difference. We all make a difference and we all have a responsibility towards society. We need to be educated for that.

We also all make a difference in the world of our own households as well as in the wider world too. For example, what we do with that plastic bottle, that's if we've chosen to buy one, makes as much difference as what the council does with its rubbish tip. We all have small individual responsibilities plus global planetary responsibility and we need to be educated for that.

Then there are our own personal gifts and skills and knowledge to develop as they may one day contribute to the discovery of a cure of a terrible disease or, equally valuable, contribute to the important work of collecting the rubbish, tending the elderly, nursing the sick. It is all of equal importance to our society, and there is really no hierarchy in terms of the difference we can make, large or small, glamorous or not. Everyone needs to be educated to make this kind of difference. And if everybody was, if everybody – every child – could see the value of their own contribution, however small, we would have children with higher self-esteem. Children with high self-esteem, children who feel that they matter, tend not to be the ones who harm themselves or others, or do damage to the world, for they see the value in good actions. That must be part of what education is for.

Education is surely not only for getting lots of qualifications or a high income. It is about valuing oneself and what one can offer and valuing others. Do our children think of themselves in those terms when they are in school? Do they see themselves as a responsible and valuable member of society and guardian of the planet? Does the education we provide, and climate in schools, encourage our children to see themselves in that way? For it is not merely academic training that gives children those skills and sense of responsibility. It is a caring education that is about raising humane and caring people.

Education is about individuals and the difference they can make. Education helps us live together responsibly, care for one another, be humane. And take our human responsibility towards the planet seriously so that other generations can enjoy it too. Education is first and foremost about humankind. It is people who are important and what those people can do. Education is for doing, not just for having.

It is these wider views that we perhaps need to embrace when thinking about education, what it is and what it is for. These wider views help us see beyond education for qualifications only, or higher income only, to seeing it as a self-valuing, life-enhancing process to enjoy and expand on forever.

*

By valuing each individual we can create a valuable education.

*

What parents might consider success to be

Success has been mentioned before in this book, how success and happiness are bound up with each other and how education and happiness are integral to each other too.

What our society considers success to be seems to change with every decade. Success in a depressed time meant having a job, or being able to read and write. Success during the war meant survival. Success during the late 1980s was very much bound up with having and acquisitions. Success in education has increasingly been measured by having lots and lots of GCSEs and A levels at A*.

So where will it end? Do we want to grind more and more qualifications out of our children at the expense of all else? For that seems to be what is in danger of happening. Yet it does not appear to be working that well for many children who 'end' their education disenchanted, disempowered in that they are unable to take charge of their lives, and dissatisfied with their prospective future. Some children without qualifications or poor basic skills are written off as having no future at all.

Apparently there is an increasing percentage of adults who are doing work that bears no relation to their degree. And there seem to be increasing numbers of entrepreneurs who took no degree at all but appear to be doing quite well for themselves, which is making people ask 'what was it all for?' A comment we hear quite often is 'I learned more after I left school', suggesting that people learn more after their so-called education has ended. Which is just the point: education is not just for a person between the ages of 5 and 18, possibly 21. Education goes on forever as we grow and change, develop and experience, and move through different phases of our lives.

If our young people have an attitude to education as a life-enhancing, life-long process, which they can utilise at any time in their life, which it surely is, then it must be a better outcome for them than one where they are desperate to get out of the school door and for it to end. That attitude would not appear to be a very successful outcome of their education.

If our definition of a successful education is based on it being for the purpose of external gain like a big house, posh car, lots of foreign holidays, then it has less chance of being achieved than if our definition included more intrinsic successes that begin closer to home and heart. Like, possibly, fulfilment in work, finding work that makes a person feel good, warm loving relationships, food and shelter.

These definitions do not preclude each other. But many parents encourage their children down the road of intensive academic gain by promise of a high income as if that was the only criteria for success. And as many highly paid professionals are finding out, it is not.

You might like to consider again the question: what is it we actually wish for our children?

Some parents never get beyond wishing for lots of measurable achievements that they can flaunt in their social circles or which keeps them up with everyone else, regardless of whether that is suitable for their own individual child. Others are looking at success as measurable by things in their children such as:

- confidence
- a sense of who they are
- a happy childhood and happy relationships with others
- understanding of their own gifts and strengths and how to use them
- good health and well-being and how to maintain it
- fulfilling work that they enjoy
- the self-esteem to get where they want to go
- lack of fear and inhibition
- the ability to tackle challenges
- to have the skills to fit in and function in the world contentedly and responsibly
- being a loving caring human being.

Looking at these outcomes as criteria for success brings a different view of the success we might be educating our children towards. It offers a completely different purpose for education. It also brings it right down to the individual, rather than something that is general, at the same time acknowledging that the individual is part of a society towards which they have a responsibility. It also prevents us educating for average, or for the masses. For is there such a thing as an average child? And would we consider an unhappy individual to be a successful one? Happy individuals all together make a happy society.

How to keep an open view and an individual view that relates to your child

Sometimes parents find that when home educating it is best not to look too far ahead. There is no foretelling what the future might be and it is sometimes easier and more successful to work with an open-ended view and in direct relation to the individual at the time.

If a child's education was always based on criteria for long-term success, whatever that might be, there would be a danger of overlooking elements of the child's personality and characteristics, strengths and abilities right now that are bound to affect it. And these will change as the child grows; therefore it is almost impossible to predict what might be best for their future.

If education instead is based on their day-to-day interests and needs, incorporating a wide experience of skills they need to develop both for now and the future, wherever they end up going will happen more naturally and more in tune with them. It could be looked at a little like that old saying 'take care of the pennies and the pounds take care of themselves'. Equally, take care of the individual child and the future takes care of itself.

Home educating is an enormous act of faith. But actually, putting children through school is equally an enormous act of faith. There is no telling whom they will come up against or what their school experience will be. At least with home educating there is much more opportunity to provide for the child as an individual. And it is that provision that will guide them towards a successful future.

Keeping as open a view as possible is the way to relate education to the individual child. An open view is one that:

- does not restrict itself to the boundaries of a traditional educational model
- does not have a generalised view of children
- embraces the alternative ways there are to learn
- loses the constraints of time, place, age or group in relation to learning
- keeps personal development at its heart and as its aim
- remains flexible and open-ended rather than purely outcome led.

Granted, this view and approach is not always easy to maintain in a society where a measurable education seems to be the only one that is held up as valid, and members of that society argue that an academic way is the only way to enter the working world. But actually, it is not. It is in some circumstances, perhaps, but not all. There are many young people already proving that, young people who are joining the world of work having been home educated with their personal development in mind, rather than only their academic achievement in mind. Young people who have been educated solely for the intrinsic value of education in itself, rather than simply for an outcome.

These young people who have gone before, and families who have successfully home educated, are proof that other ways work besides school ways and are the reassurance we need to help us keep faith with a more open-ended view and broader approach that might suit our own individual children.

Our son was very unhappy throughout his primary school and the whole experience was gruelling. At that time we had no idea that we could home educate. We battled on without empathy or support for either his dyslexia or Attention Deficit Disorder (ADD).

It was just as bad when he went to secondary school. Then I found Education Otherwise on the Internet and decided to bring him out of school. I initially thought home educating meant me teaching him so I stayed up at night preparing lessons. But he couldn't bear me pushing him into things and after talking to another home educator she persuaded me to let go of this approach and step back.

Although I found this hard I managed it to a certain extent, encouraging him to have a fun time, taking him to outings and meeting up with other home educators, but he watched an awful lot of TV and played on the computer for much of his time. He was also out and about with his many friends.

Amazingly, despite me stepping back and not structuring his time, he must have learned something, for he then went on to study A levels at college and got very good grades. He was accepted to do A levels without the necessary GCSEs. In fact when we talked to the interviewing tutor the tutor was fascinated with home educated children and said that he thought schools just produced robots!

He is now at university. They too accepted him with open arms, as they were also pleased to welcome home educated children.

Schools had basically written off my son. Yet even though he did seemingly little over the five years home educating, he still obtained three good A levels, finding the work quite easy, and is loving university. I doubt this would have been the outcome if he had remained at school.

Parent of one child, home educating for five years

Educating for intrinsic value rather than for outcome

Taking care of the child right now and letting the future take care of itself, for the larger part of their education, is a way to educate for intrinsic value rather than just for outcome.

We have, of course, always got to keep one eye on the future. Parents would not be human if they did not worry about it. But worry does not always change things. Taking action that is needed right now does.

Most of all, simply loving and respecting a human being of whatever age is more important than training them for a future that may not happen. Loved and respected children have the greatest chance of being loving and respectful adults. Self-respecting adults make education part of their life.

Some of the ways in which children are treated as part of their education does not involve respect, or even humaneness. One parent told me that her small child was denied water to drink at school. As a farmer, this parent was not even allowed to deny their milking cows access to water as there were laws to protect the cows. It seems in some cases we treat our livestock better than we treat our children, but then cows make money.

Education has a personal value to each and every one of us on a day-to-day basis, whatever age we are. But I guess few children understand that. They see it more as something boring they have to do for the adults in their life rather than for themselves. If children understand what a rich, exciting, life-building opportunity education is, for themselves and not for adults, then why would they not want to become educated? But they would certainly rebel against an education that has agendas external to them like teacher or parent pleasing, school statistics, social one-upmanship or vote winning for example. This is not an education that has an intrinsic value to them at all. Your child's education is about your child. That's where intrinsic value begins and ends.

We all need to understand that education is part of caring for oneself. It is for life. It is for a happy life. It is for the soul and the spirit as well as the head. It must be for the intrinsic good of the individual first and foremost and in order for that individual to have an impact worldwide. It is for building good and happy lives. What else really would it be for?

In the end

> We have met a great many home educated teenagers now who are all finding their own personal way forward. Some at university or college, or continuing home based learning, others working or in new apprenticeships. What I haven't yet found is a disaffected young person who feels the need to join a gang, become involved in crime or violence. Despite all the dire warnings, they can read and write, and then some!
>
> ... With hindsight I always advise new home educators not to worry too much, the kids will be fine! At one point I was accused of overprotecting my kids, but I never felt this was the case. They had a great many more natural freedoms than the freedom to go and sit in a classroom all day long! Now, those same parents, without exception, have come through the other side of the education system with huge regrets and have told me they wished they did the same thing.
>
> Obviously there are certain sacrifices – for us it has been income as we live on very little. What I think we have gained is a close relationship with our kids, we have had time with them that can never be replaced once gone, and they have experienced the freedom of learning and growing without fear and with substantially less pressure to conform, achieve, etc. The result is that they have found their talents...
>
> Parent of two children, home educating for ten years

Home education can lead families wherever they want it to go. That is the beauty of doing it. Decisions parents make about their child's education can be in line with schooling, or it can be completely independent of schooling. Both approaches work. Whatever does not work can be changed.

When children step over the school threshold they are pointed towards an academic outcome right from the outset and groomed for it with little regard to whether it works for them or not, to what makes them happy or not, or what they can bring to it themselves. This works for some families. For others it does not work and those children lose out on a wealth of alternatives that may well have suited them better and made them happier. In fact, that experience for them could be described as travelling the world by train but never seeing out the windows. What a waste that would be. Too often education becomes a similar track-led experience, one which children can't wait to step off.

Home education can be a straight track process or a worldwide one. It can be outcome led or child led. It can be curriculum led or tailor-made. But in the end, it is the opportunity for families to make the education of their children a happy and fulfilling experience, one built on respect, which nurtures their natural love of learning, develops confidence and self-esteem. An opportunity to show children that education is just for them, wholly for them, for their hearts and their souls as well as for their minds, a life-enhancing personal process, one that shows how to make the best of success and happiness, both now and for ever after.

Summary of the main points

- Home educated children integrate back into mainstream education if and when they choose to do so, or equally well into work.

- Parents need to keep in mind their children's short- and long-term needs when thinking ahead.

- Children are very able to contribute to these discussions about their education.

- Education is most importantly about the personal development of the individual.

- There are far more elements to success than simply academic qualifications; personal skills are equally important.

- Keeping an open-minded view of education helps parents to better relate education to their individual child.

- Education is a personal process available to each individual for life, not just for school.

- There is no reason why home educated children cannot get wherever they want to go.

Three thought-provoking websites to finish off with

Infed: www.infed.org

Edge Foundation: www.edge.co.uk

A.S. Neill's Summerhill School: www.summerhillschool.co.uk

Index